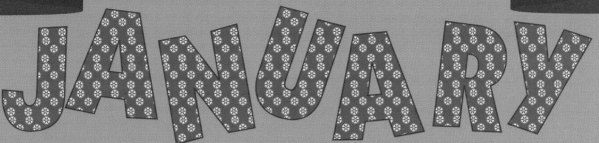

From Your Friends At The MAILBOX® *magazine*

JANUARY

A MONTH OF IDEAS AT YOUR FINGERTIPS!

GRADES 1–3

WRITTEN BY
Sherri Beckwith, Stacie Stone Davis, Michele Gunther,
Susan Hohbach, Cynthia Holcomb, Susie Kapaun, Nancy Matthews,
Sharon Murphy, Kelly O'Connor, Doug L. Poage, Kathy Wolf

EDITED BY
Lynn Bemer Coble, Carol Rawleigh, Jennifer Rudisill,
Gina Sutphin, Kathy Wolf

ILLUSTRATED BY
Jennifer Bennett, Cathy Spangler Bruce, Pam Crane,
Sheila Krill, Gary Mohrman, Rebecca Saunders, Barry Slate

TYPESET BY
David Jarrell, Lynette Maxwell

COVER DESIGNED BY
Jennifer Bennett

©1996 by THE EDUCATION CENTER, INC.
All rights reserved except as here noted.
ISBN #1-56234-125-1

Manufactured in the United States

10 9 8 7 6 5 4 3 2

TABLE OF CONTENTS

The airplane

January Calendar

Oatmeal Month

January is Oatmeal Month, and what better way to stay warm than with a bowl of hot, tasty oatmeal? Students enjoy oatmeal for cereal in the morning, in cookies for a snack, and in breads and muffins any time of day. Encourage students to bring recipes from home that use oatmeal as an ingredient, and do some cooking with your children! Write to the Quaker Oats Company, c/o Oatmeal Month, P.O. Box 530, Barrington, IL 60011, or call (312) 629-1234 for more information.

Eye Care Month

Eye Care Month was established to educate the public on preventative eye care and early detection of problems that can lead to blindness. (January 4 is the birthday of Louis Braille, who developed a touch system of reading and writing for the blind. If possible, provide a sample of Braille writing for students to examine.) Have the school nurse visit the class to discuss eye care and safety rules, and explain what is involved in a visit to the eye doctor for a checkup. Follow up by reading the story *Glasses—Who Needs 'Em?* by Lane Smith (Puffin Books, 1995).

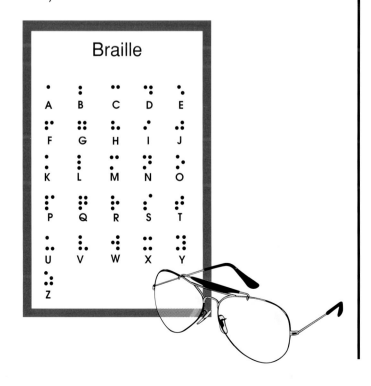

Braille

11—International Thank-You Day

This day is set aside to thank someone who has done something nice for you. Let your students take time to thank some of the people who help them every day at school. Have them write letters or make cards for cafeteria workers, custodians, secretaries, the nurse, and the librarian. Encourage them to say "Thank you" every time someone does something nice for them today!

15—Dr. Martin Luther King, Jr.'s Birthday

Honor the birthday of this civil rights leader and Nobel Peace Prize winner by having students focus on the value of respect for others. Have students ever felt discriminated against because they are children? Have they ever been ignored by an adult, or treated as if they were unimportant? Have they ever treated a younger student that way? Make students aware they have the power to cause others to feel good or bad about themselves. See the unit on pages 16–27 for ideas and information about Dr. King.

18—Pooh Day

What is celebrated on Pooh Day? A. A. Milne's birthday and his tales of Winnie the Pooh and friends. Share selections from *Winnie The Pooh*, *The House At Pooh Corner*, and *When We Were Very Young* (Puffin Books, 1992) with your class. They are sure to enjoy the exploits of the lovable bear who has an incurable craving for honey! Have a Pooh Day complete with honey-flavored Teddy Grahams™.

3

21—National Hugging Day™

We all enjoy a hug, whether it's hugging our teddy bear during a thunderstorm or hugging Grandmother when she comes for a visit. Have each student make a coupon book good for ten big hugs. Have her give coupons to friends and family members to cash in when they feel the need for an embrace. Show your students how huggable they are by giving each one a Hershey's Hug™. You are certain to make their day a little sweeter!

22—National School Nurse Day (Annually the fourth Wednesday in January)

Here's an opportunity to invite the school nurse to talk about all that she does. Make sure that she knows how much everyone values all her hard work. Have students write acrostic poems for her using the letters in "school nurse." Decorate the poems with bandages, drawings of thermometers, and other medical symbols. Your school nurse will enjoy hearing from students when they are in good health and full of good cheer!

23—National Handwriting Day

This day honors someone famous for his handwriting—John Hancock, whose birthday is also on this day. As first signer of the Declaration of Independence, his flourish of a signature is well remembered. Introduce students to John Hancock's signature on a copy of this famous document. Encourage your students to use their best handwriting all day long, taking special care when writing their signatures. Have them sign a "Declaration of Good Handwriting" to show their commitment to the effort of legible penmanship.

31—Backwards Day—(Annually the last Friday in January)

Here's a celebration that will really turn things around! Backwards Day is a day to examine your life from an opposite point of view. Schedule the school day in reverse, so that last period is held first. Eat backwards, starting with dessert. Walk backwards to recess. Have students spell their names backwards and then try to pronounce them. For the very daring, wear your clothes backwards or inside out! This day will definitely provide a change of pace in the classroom!

CLASSROOM TIMES

Teacher: _____ Date: _____

JANUARY

Events

Reminders

Superstars

Special Thanks

Help Wanted

HELLO, NEW YEAR!

People from all over the world celebrate the first day of the calendar year, or New Year's Day. Usher in another new year with these fun and festive activities!

ideas by Sherri Beckwith and Cynthia Holcomb

Roman Rituals

New Year's festivities range from religious celebrations to midnight gatherings with noisemakers. The ancient Romans celebrated New Year's Day by giving gifts of coins imprinted with the likeness of *Janus,* the god of gates, doors, and new beginnings. Janus had two faces that looked in opposite directions—one toward the past and the other into the future. January was named for Janus, whose name is derived from the Latin word for *gate.* Ask students if they see a connection between January and the Roman god. Lead a discussion about what it would be like to be able to see into the future, as Janus could. Have each student write a letter to Janus, asking him some questions about the future.

Then create Roman coins with your students. Give each student a piece of gold wrapping paper and a six-inch circle template. Have students trace and cut out their gold coins. Using fine-point markers, have each student draw a likeness of Janus onto his coin. Display the coins and letters as a reminder that the future holds many surprises!

Colonial Traditions

American colonists in New England celebrated the new year by firing guns into the air, shouting, and cheering. Many people went "calling" on friends and neighbors who were holding an open house with food and drink. Today many people celebrate with noisemakers and still hold open house for New Year's Day.

Plan a New Year's Open House for parents and families. Prepare by making invitations with the pattern on page 12. Determine how many invitations each student needs. Have students color and cut out the patterns, then mount them on 8" x 10" construction paper. Invitations with this personal touch are sure to bring lots of visitors! (See the New Year's Open House ideas on page 11.)

Counting The Days

The coming of the new year has not always been celebrated in January. At one time it was observed during the harvest season. Christians used to celebrate the new year in March, on Annunciation Day. The ancient Romans declared January 1 to be the official beginning of the year. The Chinese, Muslims, and Jews celebrate on different dates. One reason for the variety of dates was the absence of a standard calendar. In 1600 many Western nations adopted the 12-month Gregorian calendar, which we still use today.

Familiarize your students with calendar concepts using the reproducible on page 15. Provide a copy for each student. Instruct each student to label the calendar page for January. Have him number the days, taking care to begin on the correct day and end on the 31st day. Be sure to label New Year's Day and any student birthdays in January.

Extend the lesson by providing a calendar page for each of the other months. Have students complete calendars for the entire year. When they have completed the pages, help students staple them between construction-paper covers. Have students keep these calendars in their desks to keep track of birthdays, assignments, and special upcoming events.

A.M. Or P.M.?

Midnight, or 12:00 A.M., marks the beginning of a brand-new day. This is the perfect time to discuss the concept of A.M. and P.M. with your students. Use a face clock to show students the passage of time from midnight to noon, and back to midnight. Make a chart with your students as they brainstorm a list of activities they do every day. Include activities that take place at school and at home. When several activities have been listed, ask children to identify the ones that take place in A.M. and in P.M.

To reinforce this concept, have each student use this information to make a schedule of his school day. Each student should sequence the subjects or classes in his day, then write the time followed by A.M. or P.M. Allow the students to take their schedules home so that they can share their new knowledge as well as the outlines of their busy day.

For additional practice with A.M. and P.M., use the reproducible on page14. What a timely lesson for the New Year!

We're Having A Ball!

On New Year's Eve, a crowd gathers in Times Square in New York City for a special welcome to the year. People watch expectantly as an electronically lighted ball drops during the final countdown to midnight. As the ball drops lower and lower, the excitement builds. When the ball reaches the bottom, the celebration begins.

Create a similar atmosphere in your classroom to motivate your students to reach a classroom goal, such as everyone turning in his homework, using the correct heading on papers, or reading a number of books. As they work toward the goal, lower a ball to show their progress.

To create a countdown ball, cut a large circle from craft paper. Have students decorate the ball with colorful markers, confetti, and glitter. Next use sentence strips to create a "pole" five feet high. Mark the strip in six-inch increments to make ten "steps." Mount the pole on a wall or door. Place the ball at the top of the pole.

For every day that the class meets the goal, move the ball a step lower on the pole. When the ball has dropped all the way, celebrate the students' success with a class party. Replace the ball at the top of the pole to get the ball rolling toward good work habits.

Countdown Math

Your students will enjoy working on math drills with this countdown approach. Duplicate the patterns on page 13 and program the rectangular strip with math problems. Cut along the dotted lines on the ball shape with an X-acto® knife, then thread the strip through the ball shape. As students lower the ball, new math problems are uncovered. Have each student copy the problems and answer them on a sheet of paper. When the ball has reached the bottom, the student has completed his countdown. Reward him with a ball-shaped candy to celebrate his success!

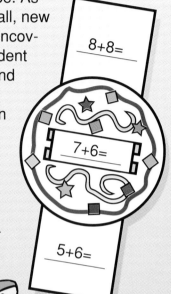

8

High-Steppin' Music

New Year's Day would not be complete without the Tournament of Roses Parade held in Pasadena, California. The tournament consists of a parade of flower-covered floats, a beauty contest, and the Rose Bowl football game. High-school bands from all over the country compete to play in this nationally televised parade.

Your students will enjoy having their own New Year's parade using instruments from your music department. If possible, invite a local high-school band director to teach your students how to march. Play some recorded marches and parade around the school grounds with your class, wishing everyone a Happy New Year.

Fabulous Floats

If an indoor parade is more your style, have students decorate minifloats for a parade display. Each student will need a shoebox and a supply of colored tissue paper to make tissue paper flowers to cover his float. To make a flower, the student takes a one-inch square of tissue paper, folds it around the eraser end of his pencil, and dabs the end with glue. The tissue square is then glued onto the shoebox. Students continue adding tissue squares until their shoeboxes are covered. When they have finished decorating their floats, have a contest. Let your students vote on the winning entry. Display the floats in the library or cafeteria for the entire school to enjoy.

Resolution Time

Many people start the New Year with resolutions to break bad habits or begin good ones. Your students are not too young to think about making resolutions! They may want to keep their desks neater, improve their spelling, or take more time with their handwriting. Encourage each student to think about habits—both good and bad—that he wants to work on, and write these down on index cards.

Create a bulletin board for students who want to share their resolutions. Mount the resolutions on construction-paper balloons. Add the title "Our New Year's Resolutions." Classmates can give each other support and encouragement as they work toward their goals. Let the students help take down the bulletin board at the end of the month and reflect on the progress they have made. Offer congratulations to those who have met with success and encouragement to those who need to keep trying.

A "Happy New Year!" For The Birds

Culminate your New Year activities with a story of sharing. *The After-Christmas Tree* by Linda Wagner Tyler (Puffin Books, 1992) tells of a young boy who is sad to see the family Christmas tree taken down. But instead of throwing it away, his family turns the tree into a treat for the wild birds and animals.

Treat your local fine-feathered friends by making bird feeders to hang outside. Set up a center with a pinecone for each student, a jar of peanut butter, plastic knives, and a bag of birdseed. Each student spreads peanut butter on his pinecone, then rolls it in birdseed. Help attach a wire or ribbon around the pinecone so that it can hang from a tree branch. To take his project home, have each student place his pinecone in a zippered plastic bag. Both the birds and the students will enjoy this activity!

New Year's Reading

Ring in the New Year by sharing these books with your class:

Ring Out, Wild Bells
written by Lee Bennett Hopkins and illustrated by Karen Baumann
(Harcourt Brace Jovanovich, Publishers; 1992)

This collection of poems honors many seasons and holidays, and features several about winter and New Year's Day.

We Celebrate New Year
written by Bobbie Kalman and illustrated by Tina Holdcroft
(Crabtree Publishing Company, 1985)

Explore New Year traditions around the world with this collection of stories, activities, and informative text.

Santa Cow Island
written by Cooper Edens and illustrated by Daniel Lane
(Green Tiger Press, 1994)

The Santa Cows are on their way to an after-Christmas vacation. They invite the Schwartz family to accompany them on the trip, which concludes with an outlandish New Year's Eve celebration.

WELCOME TO A NEW YEAR'S OPEN HOUSE!

Encourage family members to add classroom involvement to their list of New Year's resolutions!

Festive Favors

Create a festive mood at your Open House with these easy-to-make party favors. Provide each student with an empty tissue tube, two five-inch pieces of ribbon, and a ten-inch square of colored tissue paper. Fill each tube with a few pieces of wrapped candy (perhaps chocolate coins in gold foil in honor of Janus). Instruct the students to wrap the tube with tissue paper and secure the ends with ribbon. Be sure that a favor is made for every guest coming to the Open House. As each guest arrives, give him a party favor and wish him, "Happy New Year!"

You're Invited

To: _____
Date: _____
Time: _____

New Year's Open House

Class _____
Room _____

Food For Luck

In the spirit of a time-honored Southern tradition, serve up some black-eyed peas for good luck. Prepare this good-luck food the night before your Open House (see the recipe below). Provide plastic bowls and spoons. Warm your Crock-Pot® full of peas and offer a taste of good luck and prosperity for the New Year!

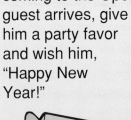 

Black-Eyed Peas
(yield—32 tasting portions)

1 cup black-eyed peas	1/2 teaspoon salt
1/4 pound salt pork	1/4 teaspoon pepper

Rinse peas in cold water. Put them in a large pot and add enough cold water to cover the peas. Cover the pot and soak the peas overnight.

In the morning, drain the peas. Put them in a six-quart saucepan with a tight-fitting lid. Chop the salt pork and add it to the peas. Add enough cold water to cover the peas.

Bring to a boil, then turn the heat to low. Cover and simmer until peas are tender, about 30 minutes. Some water will be left in the pot.

Gone, But Not Forgotten

Before moving ahead in the new year, reflect on the events that occurred in the previous year. Ask students and guests, "Did we get a new president? Did the weather make the headlines? What exciting things happened at school?" Record the responses and help the students sequence the events. Post the list in the classroom to help remember the past year. Encourage students to watch for current events on the television, radio, and in the newspaper.

As the new year progresses, make a list of newsworthy events of the brand-new year. As you add events to the list, have students compare them with things that occurred during the past year. As the list grows, your class will be in the know for the new year!

Patterns

Use with "Colonial Traditions" on page 6.

YOU'RE INVITED

To: _____

Date: _____

Time: _____

NEW YEAR'S OPEN HOUSE

_____ Class

_____ Room Number

©1996 The Education Center, Inc. • *JANUARY* • TEC196

YOU'RE INVITED

To: _____

Date: _____

Time: _____

NEW YEAR'S OPEN HOUSE

_____ Class

_____ Room Number

©1996 The Education Center, Inc. • *JANUARY* • TEC196

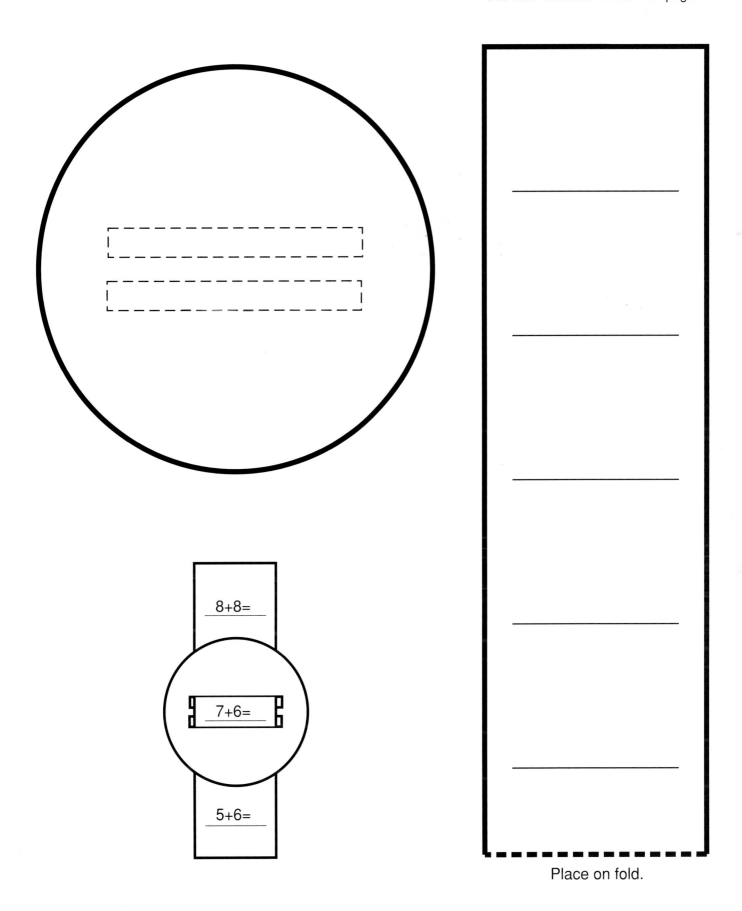

8+8=

7+6=

5+6=

Place on fold.

A.M.
Or
P.M.?

Write A.M. or P.M. to show when these things happen:

Eat breakfast _____   Eat supper _____

Go to bed _____   Go home from school _____

Get dressed for school _____   Go to lunch _____

See the sunrise _____   See the sunset _____

Tell what you are doing at:

7:00 A.M.   7:00 P.M.

_____   _____

_____   _____

_____   _____

11:00 A.M.   11:00 P.M.

_____   _____

_____   _____

_____   _____

_____
Month

Sunday	Monday	Tuesday	Wednesday	Thursday	Friday	Saturday

©1996 The Education Center, Inc. • *JANUARY* • TEC196

Note To The Teacher: Use with "Counting The Days" on page 8.

Remembering Martin Luther King, Jr.

Lead your students down the road to freedom with these cross-curricular activities to celebrate Martin Luther King, Jr. Day!

ideas by Doug Poage and Sharon Murphy

Happy Birthday, Martin Luther King, Jr.

Your students are sure to look forward to studying Martin Luther King, Jr., when you begin your unit with a birthday party in his honor. Have them figure out how old Dr. King would be on this birthday (see the timeline on page 17). Then encourage your students to join in as you sing "Happy Birthday" to him.

Next share *Happy Birthday, Martin Luther King* by Jean Marzollo (Scholastic Inc.,1993) with your students. This easy-to-read book gives a brief account of the life of Martin Luther King, Jr. Be sure to emphasize Dr. King's dream "that people everywhere would learn to live together without being mean to one another." Ask students how Martin Luther King would want everyone in the class to treat each other. List students' responses on the board.

After discussing the book, ask your students to think of something nice they could do for their classmates or something that would help make the classroom a more pleasant place. Tell students that they are each going to write down this good deed and then wrap it as a present for Martin Luther King's birthday. Each student will need an 8" x 8" sheet of lined paper, colored construction paper, glue, and birthday wrapping paper. First have students write their good deeds on the lined pieces of paper. Next have each student glue his piece of wrapping paper to the piece of construction paper, as shown, to make a flap. Then each student staples the wrapping paper on top of the good deed at the top to make a present. As an extra touch, have each student tie a bow from yarn and glue it to the top of the present where the staple is located. Then display these beautiful presents on a bulletin board titled "Happy Birthday, Martin Luther King, Jr." Your class will enjoy lifting up the wrapping-paper flaps to reveal the good deeds.

In Step With Martin Luther King

Motivate your students to work on both their map and sequencing skills as you let them follow in Martin Luther King's footsteps. First write each of the years listed below on a sentence strip. (Be sure to include the event and location.) Provide a U.S. map and a world map large enough for all students to view at one time.

To begin the activity, mix up the sentence strips so they are not in sequential order. Next read each of the sentence strips to the class and ask your students to help you put the events in the order in which they happened. Tape the sentence strips to a piece of chart paper as students give them to you. After the class has placed the events in sequence, older students can find the locations on one of the maps.

1929 MLK was born. *(Atlanta, Georgia)*
1951 MLK graduates from seminary. *(Chester, Pennsylvania)*
1953 MLK married Coretta Scott. *(Marion, Alabama)*
1954 MLK began in his first position as a minister. *(Montgomery, Alabama)*
1955 MLK earned his doctoral degree. *(Boston, Massachusetts)*
1963 Dr. King gave his famous "I Have A Dream" speech. *(Washington,DC)*
1964 Dr. King was awarded the Nobel Peace Prize. *(Norway)*
1968 Dr. King died. *(Memphis, Tennessee)*

Peace-Prize Awards

Dr. Martin Luther King, Jr., worked very hard and gave his life for a more peaceful nation. He was honored with one of the most important prizes in the world—the Nobel Peace Prize. Each year this award is given to the person (or persons) who has (have) done the most for peace. In December of 1964, Martin Luther King was awarded this distinguished prize. He was given a medal and $54,000. He gave the money to several black organizations because he said it belonged to all Black Americans.

After sharing this information with your students, help them recognize the positive strengths in their classmates by creating Peace-Prize Awards. Duplicate one of the patterns on page 22 for each of your students. Have them color and cut out the awards. Next have each child glue the award on cardstock or construction paper and trim it, leaving a border around the award. Each child then applies glue in a design around the border of the award and sprinkles the glue with gold glitter. After the glue has dried, shake the excess glitter into a container and punch a hole at the top of each award. Then help each student thread a 24-inch piece of yarn through the hole and tie it to make a necklace.

To prepare to give out these special awards, call out a student's name. His classmates will then take turns saying something nice about him. (For example, "Juan helps others by treating then kindly.") Write down at least one good statement that was said about that student. Repeat this activity for each student. Save these statements and awards to present at the upcoming Freedom Tea (see page 20). You will be amazed at how proud your students will be at receiving the awards!

Man Of The Year

In January 1964, *Time* magazine chose Martin Luther King, Jr., to be its Man Of The Year. His face was on the cover of the magazine. If possible show your students a copy of *Time* magazine and discuss why it is an honor to be on the cover.

Then let your students create two covers for a new *Time* magazine. Give each student one sheet of 9" x 12" white construction paper. On one side of the paper the student will draw a picture of Martin Luther King, Jr., and write a sentence stating why Dr. King was chosen. On the other side of the paper, the student will draw a picture of himself and then write a sentence about what he might do in the future to get on the cover of *Time* magazine. After everyone is finished, have your students share these new magazine covers. They're hot off the presses!

Martin Luther King by peacefully protes

Korita Steverson, first black woman on the Supreme Court

Getting Some Big Words

From a very early age, Martin Luther King was fascinated with words. He once said, "When I grow up I'm going to get me some big words." Well he did. In one year alone, Dr. King gave more than 350 speeches about freedom for everyone.

Share the above statement with your students and then read the following excerpt from one of his famous speeches. He told Americans that it was his dream that...

"my four little children will one day live in a nation where they will not be judged by the color of their skin, but by the content of their character."

For vocabulary development, discuss with your students what is meant by "the content of their character." A good way to do this would be to connect the phrase to character traits such as *kindness, honesty, helpfulness,* and *respect.* Next make a copy of the reproducible titled "The Content Of Their Character" on page 23 for each student. Using the given word bank and a dictionary, if needed, have your students write the appropriate character trait in the sentence with its definition. Then have students think of character traits they have and list them, as well as traits of Martin Luther King.

We Shall Overcome

Get your students in tune as they learn the civil rights song "We Shall Overcome." Refer to *...If You Lived At The Time Of Martin Luther King* by Ellen Levine (Scholastic Inc., 1990) for the words of the song. Before the singing starts, share with your students the following information about Martin Luther King:

- Dr. King spent his life leading the movement for Black Americans to be treated equally and fairly.
- Dr. King used only peaceful, nonviolent types of actions.
- He led a bus boycott, freedom marches, and sit-ins.
- Dr. King and his followers marched to the song "We Shall Overcome." The song tells people not to give up.

To teach your students the words to this song, write the words on chart paper. After reading the words and then singing the song, discuss what Dr. King wanted to "overcome." Then ask students to brainstorm some hardships or changes that they have had to overcome in their lives, such as moving to a new school and making new friends or learning how to read. List what students have had to overcome on the board. Have each student choose one obstacle he has overcome and write a short story about it. Be sure to have students share their stories with the class so students can acknowledge each other for their accomplishments. Save these stories to share at the Freedom Tea (see page 20).

Memory Booklets

Here's a booklet to help your students remember facts about Martin Luther King. Reproduce the booklet cover and pages on pages 26 and 27 for each child. Have the students cut them out, sequence them, and staple them together on the left-hand side. After reading through the booklets with your students, ask them to write a response to the question on the last page. Be sure to keep these memory booklets to share with parents and friends at your upcoming Freedom Tea (see page 20).

7

Would Martin Luther King think today's world was peaceful? Why or why not?

I think Martin Luther King would not think the world is peaceful. There is a lot of crime in the cities. Also many people have guns and break the law.

19

Freedom Tea

At the end of your unit on Martin Luther King, invite parents to school for a Freedom Tea. Reproduce the invitation on page 22 for your students to fill in, cut out, decorate, and take home. Ask some parents to provide tea and cookies for refreshments.

Several days prior to the event, make one copy of "Facts for the Freedom Tea" on pages 24 and 25. Cut the strips apart and assign one fact to each student to memorize for a choral speaking at the tea.

Prior to your guests' arrival, have the memory booklets (see page 19) and the "We Shall Overcome" stories (see page 19) out on the tables. As your guests arrive, suggest that they enjoy these booklets and stories. When everyone has arrived, have your students line up around the room and say their memorized lines. Then have your students join hands and sing "We Shall Overcome." At the conclusion of your event, present the "Peace-Prize Awards" (see page 17) to each member of the class and serve the refreshments.

A "Dreamful" Of Good Reading

The Story Of Ruby Bridges
by Robert Coles
(Scholastic Inc., 1995)

This moving story portrays the hostility of segregation seen through the eyes of a six-year-old girl named Ruby Bridges. Ruby was the first African-American girl to integrate Frantz Elementary School in New Orleans in 1960. She found herself surrounded by prejudice and hatred.

After sharing this story about this important event in American history, discuss the following thought-provoking questions and statements:

- How do you think Ruby felt at first about moving to New Orleans?
- Why couldn't Ruby go to any school she wanted?
- How did Ruby's parents feel about her going to this new school?
- Describe Ruby's first day at her new school.
- Compare Ruby's first day of school to your first day of school.
- How did Ruby's teacher feel about her?
- Do you think Ruby was scared to go to school every day?
- Describe Ruby's character.

When your students are finished answering the questions and following the directions, read the afterword at the end of the story. It lets the reader know what became of Ruby Bridges.

Martin Luther King / Both / Students

liked to play hide-and-seek

Both friendly, loved to read

Students like to roller-blade

Martin Luther King, Jr.: A Biography For Young Children
by Carol Hilgartner Schlank and Barbara Metzger
(Gryphon House, Inc.; 1990)

This book is a biography of Dr. Martin Luther King, Jr., that was written especially for younger children. It gives a good account of what Martin's life was like as a child. It describes his crusade for equality for Black Americans as he got older.

After reading this story to your students, discuss Martin Luther King's childhood. Ask them to compare his childhood to their own childhoods. Draw a large Venn diagram, as shown, on the board to record their responses. Students will enjoy comparing themselves to the great Martin Luther King, Jr.

Martin Luther King, Jr.
by Kathie Billingslea Smith
(Simon & Schuster, Inc.; 1987)

This biography gives the details of Martin Luther King's interesting life—presenting them so students in the primary grades can understand. After reading it, refer back to the pages in the book that mention the *bus boycott, sit-ins,* and *marches.* Starting with the bus boycott, briefly explain each term. When the students have a good understanding of each term, ask them to pretend that their favorite fast-food restaurant has decided that children are not allowed to sit down while they are eating. Only adults can sit down. Most students will think that is not fair. Have your students work in groups of three to design signs that they could carry if they were going to hold a protest march. Be sure to display their signs around your room.

Kids Have Equal Rights

Pattern
Use with "Peace-Prize Awards" on page 17.

Invitation
Use with "Freedom Tea" on page 20.

 **You Are Invited To Our Freedom Tea!**

Where: _____

When: _____

Come and celebrate with us as we follow in Martin Luther King's footsteps.

22

"The Content Of Their Character"

Use the word bank to write the correct word in each blank. Look up each word you don't know in a dictionary.

Word Bank

peaceful   helpful   polite   honest   risk taker   conscientious

1. A person who takes chances is a _____.
2. A person who helps others is _____.
3. Someone who is calm and doesn't like fighting is _____.
4. A _____worker always does his best work.
5. A person who uses good manners is called _____.
6. Someone who tells the truth is called _____.

In the spaces below, write four character traits that describe Martin Luther King and four character traits that describe you. Draw a picture of yourself in the frame.

Martin Luther King, Jr.

You

_____   _____

_____   _____

_____   _____

_____   _____

Bonus Box: On the back of this sheet, use a dictionary to help you write some other words that describe yourself.

Note To The Teacher: Use with "Getting Some Big Words" on page 18.

Facts For the Freedom Tea

1. Thank you for coming. We are going to tell you a little bit about Martin Luther King, Jr.

2. Martin Luther King, Jr., was born on January 15, 1929, in Atlanta, Georgia.

3. He studied hard in school and did very well.

4. He loved to read books.

5. He enjoyed listening to his father preach.

6. Martin Luther King, Jr., graduated from college in 1948.

7. Then he went to study in Pennsylvania to be a preacher.

8. In 1953 Martin married Coretta Scott.

9. For awhile they lived in Boston, where Martin was in graduate school.

10. Then they decided to go back to the South and help other blacks.

11. In May of 1954, Martin became a preacher at a church in Montgomery, Alabama.

12. He wanted to help people understand that a person's skin color is not important.

Note To The Teacher: Use these with "Freedom Tea" on page 20.

13. In 1955 Martin received another degree. Then he was called Dr. King.

14. Dr. King had a dream that all people would be treated equally.

15. Dr. King chose nonviolent ways to try to make a difference.

16. He led a bus boycott, sit-ins, and protest marches.

17. He gave many speeches.

18. His most famous speech is the "I Have A Dream" speech that he gave in Washington, DC.

19. Dr. King and his followers marched and sang the civil rights song "We Shall Overcome."

20. In 1964 Dr. King won the Nobel Peace Prize.

21. Congress soon made new laws for everyone.

22. In 1968 Dr. King was shot and killed in Memphis, Tennessee.

23. Dr. King's birthday is now a federal holiday.

24. We celebrate his birthday every year on the third Monday of January.

25. We will always remember Martin Luther King, Jr., for working so hard to solve problems in peaceful ways.

My Memory Book of Martin Luther King, Jr.

By _____

1

Martin Luther King, Jr., was born on January 15, 1929. He worked hard in school.

2

After graduating from college, he went to school to become a preacher. He married Coretta Scott.

3

King's first work as a preacher was in Alabama. He wanted to help people understand that all people are important, no matter what color they are.

Note To The Teacher: Use with "Memory Booklets" on page 19.

4

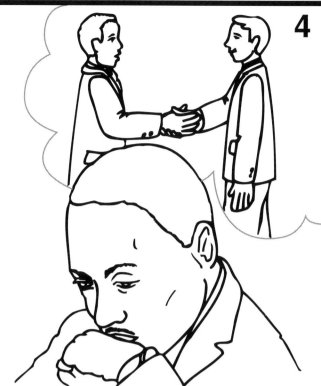

Dr. King gave speeches all around this country. He had a dream that one day all people would be treated equally.

5

He taught people to use words and peaceful actions, not fists, to solve their problems. In 1964 Dr. King won the Nobel Peace Prize.

6

In 1968 Dr. King was shot and killed. We celebrate his birthday every year because he worked hard to make his dream of peace come true.

7

Would Martin Luther King think today's world was peaceful? Why or why not?

Note To The Teacher: Use with "Memory Booklets" on page 19.

Making A Splash With...WHALES!

Make a splash in your classroom with this unit on the largest member of the animal kingdom! Your students can be practicing basic skills while whale watching.

ideas by Susie Kapaun and Cynthia Holcomb

What Is A Whale?

Dive into your study of whales with a class brainstorming session. Have each student name one large animal. Record each answer on the board. After each student has answered, have the class rank the animals from smallest to largest. Now you can reinforce that the whale is the largest animal on Earth. Some students may be surprised that the whale belongs in the mammal family and not in the fish family. Share the information below. Then provide the reproducible on page 41 for students to complete.

• Whales are warm-blooded mammals.
• A mother whale bears one live calf and nurses her offspring with milk.
• Whales have hair (although only a few stiff strands on the head).
• Whales breathe with lungs.
• The whale has a highly developed brain.
• Whales, dolphins, and porpoises all belong to the same order of animals known as *cetaceans.*
• There are two major subgroups of whales—baleen whales, of which there are ten, and toothed whales (including dolphins and porpoises), numbering 68.

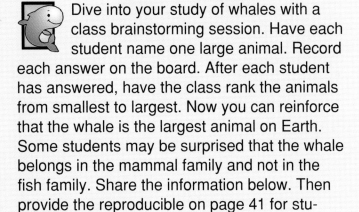

• Toothed whales actively hunt their food and have one blowhole.
• Baleen whales strain their food, have two blowholes, and are generally larger in size.

A Whale Of A Chart

Let students help set the direction of study by creating a whale chart. Have students think of facts they already know about whales. Record their responses on chart paper that has been labeled with these categories: "Whale Facts," "Whale Opinions," and "Whale Questions." Continue by recording opinions they have about whales and questions about whales that they would like to have answered during the unit. Record their responses under the correct headings.

Display the chart in the room so that the class can refer to it during each lesson. Not only will your class feel as though they have an active part in this unit, but it will allow you to reinforce facts and opinions about whales.

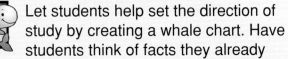

Whale Facts	Whale Opinions	Whale Questions
1. They are not fish.	1. They are cute.	1. Do they sleep?
2. They have lungs.	2. They are the scariest animal.	2. How do they find food?
		3. What are their enemies?

Staying Afloat

Students may wonder how such a large, heavy animal as the whale can stay afloat in the ocean. These two activities will reinforce two important concepts:

— Salt water, being more dense than fresh water, helps objects to float.
— Whale fat, or *blubber,* is buoyant in water.

The first activity will demonstrate the density of salt water. You may want to demonstrate this to the class or have them work in groups as you give them the directions.

You will need:
2 clear glasses
water
salt
food coloring
a crayon or plastic figure that barely sinks in
   fresh water
2 tablespoons of lard

Begin by pouring one cup of water into each glass. In one glass, mix two teaspoons of salt. Put a few drops of food coloring into the saltwater mixture, so that you will be able to tell it apart from the fresh water.

Now place an object into the fresh water and observe how it sinks. Try it again using the saltwater mixture, and observe how the object stays afloat.

Extend the activity by adding a tablespoon of lard to each glass of water. Have the students observe that the lard is very buoyant, like a whale's blubber.

The Benefits Of Blubber

Point out to students that most mammals have thick hair to hold heat next to their bodies. Since a whale's hair is sparse, blubber is its way to keep warm in the cold ocean temperatures. Whale blubber is found in a layer beneath the skin. It can be from 6 to 20 inches thick!

Help your students discover what a good insulator blubber is firsthand by slipping on a blubber glove. The glove is easy to make using two Ziploc® sandwich bags, 1 1/2 cups of lard, and strong tape.

Begin by filling one sandwich bag with the lard. Then, turning the other bag inside out, place it inside the first bag. Zip the two together. To reinforce the seal, use strong tape around the Ziploc® edges. Put your hand inside the glove to spread the lard around evenly inside the bags. Have each student test the insulating property of blubber by placing his bare hand in a bowl of ice water at the same time as he places his gloved hand into the bowl. Which stays warmer? Help students conclude that besides helping them to float, blubber keeps whales warm.

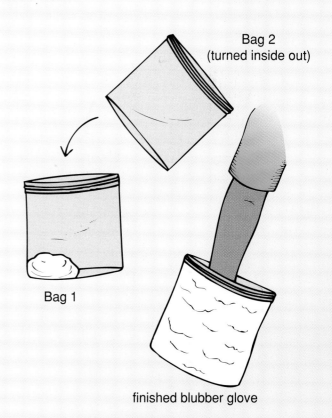

Bag 2
(turned inside out)

Bag 1

finished blubber glove

Going To Great Lengths

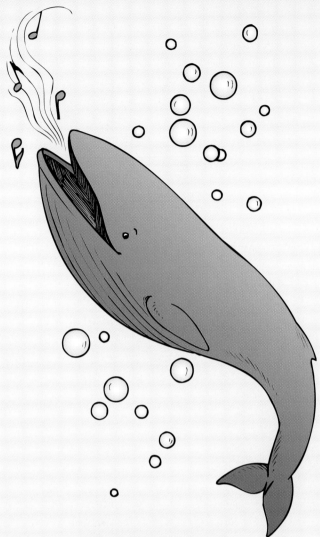

Challenge your students with this lengthy math activity that's sure to have them thinking in yards. Create a starting point in the hall or in the gymnasium. From there measure these lengths:

Narwhal	15 ft.
Killer whale	24 ft.
Minke whale	33 ft.
Gray whale	45 ft.
Right whale	57 ft.
Bowhead whale	60 ft.
Fin whale	72 ft.
Blue whale	100 ft.

Mark each length in order from smallest to largest with a piece of masking tape and then write the name of each cetacean from page 42 on each piece of tape.

Divide students into groups of three. Each person in the group will need a copy of the reproducible on page 42 and a yardstick. To keep track of how many lengths there are from the starting point to each marker, students should write the number three each time the yardstick is moved. Once your students have gone the distance, have them compare and complete their worksheets.

King Of The Ocean

Blue whales are considered to be the largest creatures to have ever lived, weighing in at over 100 tons and reaching lengths of more than 100 feet. Celebrate the size of this enormous whale with this song sung to the tune of "The Adventures Of Kookaburra."

Blue whale swims in the deep, dark sea,
Largest mammal known to you and me.
Swim, blue whale, swim, blue whale…
What an enormity!

Blue whale swims in the deep, dark sea,
King of the ocean is he.
Swim, blue whale, swim, blue whale…
What an enormity!

Name That Whale!

Wow your students with the exciting task of identifying whales. Gather several reference books such as *Whales, Dolphins, And Porpoises* by Mark Carwardine (Dorling Kindersley, 1992). Using index cards, write the name of a different cetacean on each one. Have students work together in pairs, selecting a card and locating information pertaining to that particular mammal. Provide partners with a sheet of 12" x 18" white construction paper to fold in half. On the left side, have students write information about their whale including the name of the whale, its size, its weight, and whether it is a toothed or baleen whale. On the right half, have youngsters draw a picture of the whale they chose. Allow students to share their information with their classmates. Then display the finished reports all around your classroom for the whale-watching activity at right.

Blue Whale

100 feet long
100 tons
baleen

We're Going On A Whale Watch

Whale watchers are able to identify the type of whale by watching it exhale. When a whale comes to the surface to breathe, it opens its nostrils, or *blowhole,* for about two seconds. When the whale exhales, it produces a cloud of water vapor called a *spout,* or *blow.* Experts can identify the species of whale by watching the spout. *Humpbacks* have a spout of about six feet. *Sperm whales* can spout 25 feet. They blow forward and then to the left. The *right whale* will have a V-shaped spout, while some other *baleen whales* will have a pear-shaped one.

Before you set out on your expedition, you'll want each child to make a pair of binoculars from 9" x 12" tagboard that has been cut into fourths. Each youngster rolls and glues the tagboard to make two tubes. Then tape the tubes side by side as shown. Punch a hole on the outside of each tube and attach a string for the neck strap. Have students decorate the outside of their binoculars as they choose.

Next mount the students' whale projects from above and label each wall in your room with the appropriate cardinal directions. After donning their decorative binoculars, send your students on a Whale Watch. Give each student a sheet of writing paper for recording his findings, including the name of the whale and where it was spotted. For example, a child might write, "I spotted a killer whale on the south wall next to the bookcase." Allow individuals to share their findings—you'll find they've learned a lot about whales and following directions!

1

2

3

"Hello-lo-lo-lo"

You're sure to make a big splash with this echolocation activity—a variation of the child's game Marco Polo. Explain to your students that many whales navigate and find food by making noises. By the return of the sound, the *echo,* they can tell if something is close by or farther away depending on the amount of time it takes for the echo to return.

To play this large group game, you will need a blindfold for the player who is the Whale. All other participants are Whale Food. Take your class to the gym or cafeteria where the players can set up stationary positions and the Whale will have room to move around. Or, if weather permits, play outside. Set boundaries so that the Whale Food doesn't escape all of the Whales.

To play, the blindfolded player makes a sound simulating that of a whale. The other players must immediately echo that sound. In turn, the Whale repeats the noise, following the echoes until contact with another player is made. That player then becomes the Whale.

Whimsical Whales

Teach whale anatomy with this art project. Begin by drawing the body of a whale on the board. Advise your students that you will need their assistance in the completion of this whale. Ask students what parts are missing. Encourage students to use the proper terminology as they add missing parts to the whale. Label the additions: *dorsal fin, flukes, flipper, blowhole, eye,* and *spout.* Now that your anatomy lesson is complete, your youngsters can create their own three-dimensional whales. Supply each student with a white paper lunch sack, two pages from a newspaper, a twist-tie or rubber band, a piece of tagboard, scissors, and half of a piece of 9" x 12" white construction paper.

To begin have students lightly crumple their newspaper and stuff their paper bags with it. Next demonstrate how to twist the open end of the bag closed and secure it with the twist-tie or rubber band, forming the tail. Have your students glue on flukes, flippers, and dorsal fins cut from tagboard. Allow students to paint their whales using gray tempera paint and sponges or paintbrushes.

As the whales are drying, have each child take the construction paper and roll it into a cylinder. Next have him twist the bottom and cut slits from the top about three-quarters of the way down. This forms the spout. Once his whale is completely dry, have him poke a hole where the blowhole should be and push the twisted end of the spout in so that it stands upright. Using a black marker, the student adds the eyes. You now have a pod of whimsical whales to display on a table or bookshelf.

Whale Tales

Scientists who keep records of humpback whales identify them by the markings on their flukes. Share this fact with your class, and display photos of distinctive whale flukes if possible. Have each student design a whale's flukes with a unique pattern to set the stage for a creative-writing assignment.

Give each student a piece of 9" x 12" white construction paper. Have him draw the outline of a whale's flukes above water as shown and create unique markings. Then, using black and white crayons, the student colors in the flukes, pressing hard while coloring. Using diluted light blue tempera paint, he paints over the whole page, producing a crayon resist.

Ask students to create names for their whales. Then challenge your students to write a story using the whale they just designed as the main character. Post student stories with their flukes on a bulletin board titled "Whale Tales." Your students will learn that successful writing is no fluke!

Whale Wise

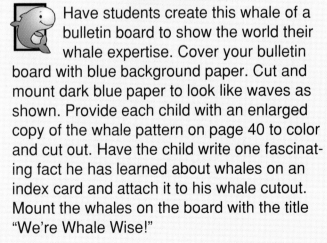

Have students create this whale of a bulletin board to show the world their whale expertise. Cover your bulletin board with blue background paper. Cut and mount dark blue paper to look like waves as shown. Provide each child with an enlarged copy of the whale pattern on page 40 to color and cut out. Have the child write one fascinating fact he has learned about whales on an index card and attach it to his whale cutout. Mount the whales on the board with the title "We're Whale Wise!"

An Incredible Journey

Explain to students that humpback whales migrate between cold, arctic waters and warm, tropical waters depending on the season. Then have students follow the path that some humpbacks take. Provide each student with a copy of the map on page 43. Point out that humpbacks live in the Gulf of Alaska during the summer and travel to the Gulf of California for the winter. With cotton swabs dipped in blue tempera paint, have your youngsters track the course humpbacks take during migration by making dots connecting the two destinations.

Then share the story *Humphrey, The Lost Whale* by Wendy Tokuda and Richard Hall (Heian International, Inc.; 1992). This is the true story of a migrating whale who accidentally took a wrong turn but finally found his way back to open waters. As a follow-up to this story, have each student track Humphrey's journey on the same reproducible map with another cotton swab and red tempera paint. Remind your students that Humphrey and his friends were heading south for the winter when Humphrey lost his way.

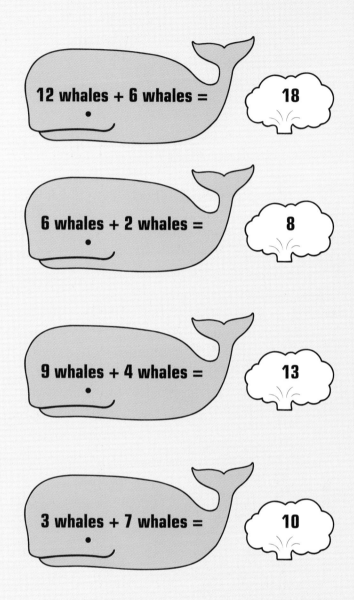

12 whales + 6 whales = 18

6 whales + 2 whales = 8

9 whales + 4 whales = 13

3 whales + 7 whales = 10

Something To Spout About

Students will really have something to spout about as they play this math game. For a fun math-fact review, duplicate 12 whales from page 40 onto light blue construction paper. Duplicate 12 spouts on white construction paper. Program each whale with a math sentence. Label the spouts with the answers. Have students play in pairs to match whales to spouts and verify each other's answers. Place the whales and spouts in a recloseable bag for storage.

Those Wacky Whales

In addition to blowing and spouting, whales do some other pretty peculiar things—and no one is quite sure why. Introduce these interesting actions performed by whales with the booklet project on pages 44–45. To complete the pages, the students cut out and glue the definitions with the corresponding actions. Next have students cut apart the resulting pages and staple them together to create wonderful whale booklets. If possible, show a video about whales and have students look for these behaviors:

- breaching—Leaping out of the water headfirst, then falling back with a splash.
- lobtailing—Slapping its flukes on the water's surface.
- flipper-slapping—Waving or slapping its flippers above the water.
- sailing—Raising the flukes high in the air and letting the wind push them.
- spyhopping—Raising the head out of the water, body in a vertical position, as though to look around.
- logging—When a group of whales rests on the water's surface, all facing the same direction.
- blow/spout—The spray of mist that forms when a whale surfaces and exhales.

Those Wacky Whales
by

©1996 The Education Center, Inc. • JANUARY • TEC1

Adopt A Whale

Engage your students in a whale awareness program. Enlighten them with the fact that many whales are endangered and that some are close to extinction due to overhunting, water pollution, and net fishing. Many institutions have been formed specifically for protecting whales. To receive more information on how your youngsters can become more involved, write to:

Pacific Whale Foundation (PWF)
Kealia Beach Plaza, Suite 25
101 N. Kihei Rd.
Kihei, HI 96753

Your class may be interested in adopting a whale through the Whale Adoption Project. To adopt a whale and receive the *Whalewatch* newsletter and the Whale Order Catalog, contact:

International Wildlife Coalition
70 East Falmouth Highway
East Falmouth, MA 02536-5954

As a whole-group writing activity, compose a letter sharing the concerns your students have about the predicament of whales today. Then have each student create a poster showing his support for saving these gentle giants. Display the posters and send copies of the letter to local newspapers and TV stations. Invite a TV news crew to interview your whale activists. Perhaps your efforts will make some waves!

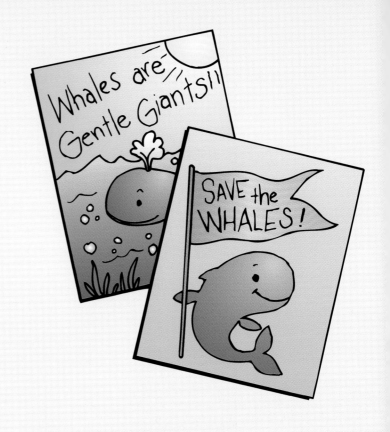

Whale Jigglers

Culminate your unit by serving these cetacean sensations! To make whale JIGGLERS®, you will need to prepare a batch of blue Jell-O® in advance according to the directions. Use a whale-shaped cookie cutter (found at your local craft store) to cut out a blue whale for each child. Help each child use a can of whipped cream to add a spout. Share your enthusiasm with your students about all the whale wisdom they have acquired.

A Whale Of A Tale

Share a tale about a whale for a lesson that's sure to be a huge success.

The Whales' Song
by Dyan Sheldon
(Dial Books For Young Readers, 1994)

This moving story tells about a girl named Lilly who longs to hear the song of the whales as her grandmother had years before. Grandma says a gift of a perfect shell or a beautiful stone might entice the whales to sing. After reading the story and sharing the wondrous illustrations by Gary Blythe, ask each student to think of what special thing he would offer the whales to hear them sing.

Then, if possible, play a tape of recorded whale songs available in bookstores. Ask students to think of words to describe these unusual sounds. Whales make sounds that have been described as whistles, clicks, gurgles, squeaks, moans, and groans. A humpback whale can make over 1,000 sounds. Its song can be heard underwater 100 miles away! Other whales sing in return. Explain that scientists think these songs are how whales communicate with each other. Ask students, "What might the whales be saying to each other?"

Have students imagine they are whales swimming in a pod. Have them write and illustrate a story from the point of view of a humpback whale. Encourage them to include dialogue between whales or with other sea creatures. Bind the stories and pictures into a class booklet titled "Whale Songs."

Whale Tales

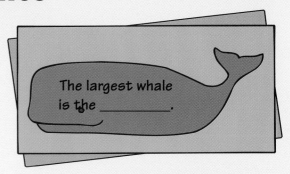

The largest whale is the _____.

Ibis: A True Whale Story

by John Himmelman
(Scholastic Inc., 1990)

Ibis is a humpback calf who, like most young-sters, is very curious. Unfortunately her inquisi-tiveness lands her in trouble. In need of rescue, Ibis is initially frightened of the people who are trying to help her. Then she relates their helping hands to something comforting…a starfish. After reading this story to your students, discuss shapes that a whale might see underwater. Brainstorm a list of different shapes. Provide each student with a large sheet of art paper and have him draw a large whale shape as shown. Next add several underwater shapes. Have students transform the shapes into underwater scenes by painting over the crayon illustrations with watercolors or watered-down blue tempera paint. Display the paintings on a bulletin board with the title "We're Taking Shape Underwater."

Three Whales Who Won The Heart Of The World

by Suzanne Kita
(Island Heritage Publishing, 1996)

This beautifully illustrated book tells of the plight of three whales that become trapped in the ice. The story begins in Hawaii and takes the reader along the migratory path the whales travel to Alaska. Thanks to the joint efforts of people from around the world, two of the three whales survive.

After sharing this remarkable true story, ask students to tell how cooperation saved the whales from total disaster. Then divide your class into cooperative groups and give each group the task of creating a trail game based on the travels of whales. Provide poster board and whale stickers for each group to design a trail as shown. Duplicate several copies of the whale pattern on page 40 for each group to write its questions on. Students can sculpt miniature whales from clay or adhere whale stickers to bottle caps for game markers. Have each group explain how to play its game to another group. This is a whale of a way to review facts.

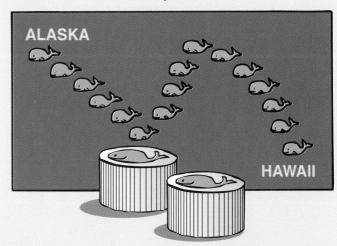

ALASKA

HAWAII

Dear Mr. Blueberry

by Simon James
(Margaret K. McElderry Books, 1991)

This amusing story is about a young girl named Emily who believes a blue whale has taken up residence in her backyard pond. This situation prompts Emily to write to Mr. Blueberry, her teacher. Use this exchange of letters to teach basic facts about whales and introduce a weeklong letter-writing activity between you and your youngsters.

After reading the story, write a letter to your students asking them for advice about the whale you found in your bathtub at home. Duplicate one copy of your letter per student, and provide them with writing paper so they may respond to your situation. Continue writing to your class for three or four days until your whale mysteriously finds its way back to the open sea.

More Whale Tales

Whales by Gail Gibbons (Holiday House, Inc.; 1991)

Baby Whales Drink Milk by Barbara Juster Esbensen (HarperCollins Children's Books, 1994)

Whales: A First Discovery Book by Editions Gallimard (Scholastic Inc., 1991)

Winter Whale by Joanne Ryder (Mulberry Books, 1994)

Whale And Dolphin by Vincent Serventy (Scholastic Inc., 1984)

Teacher Resource

Whales, The Nomads Of The Sea by Helen Roney Sattler (out of print; check your school or local library.)

Award

You Did A Whale Of A Job!

_____

made a big splash in our class by

_____

_____

Congratulations on a huge success!

Teacher: _____   **Date:** _____

©1996 The Education Center, Inc. • *JANUARY* • TEC196

39

Patterns

Use with "Whale Wise" on page 33, "Something To Spout About" on page 34, and *Three Whales Who Won The Heart Of The World* on page 38.

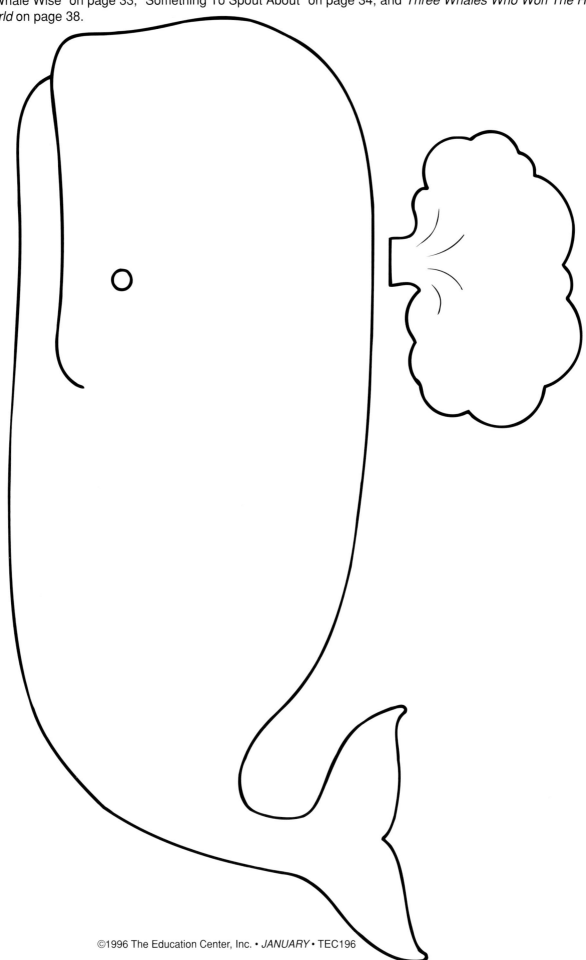

©1996 The Education Center, Inc. • *JANUARY* • TEC196

Two Kinds Of Whales

There are two main types of whales. Some whales have teeth and are called **toothed whales**. Others do not have teeth and are called **baleen whales**.

Toothed whales each have a row of teeth on the lower jaw. They use their teeth to catch fish and other animals, but they do not chew them. They swallow their food whole! Some toothed whales can taste their food, but most have a poor sense of taste. Toothed whales like to live in large groups. Most do not *migrate,* or travel, during the change in seasons. Toothed whales have one blowhole on the top of their heads.

Baleen whales do not have any teeth. Instead they have strips of baleen hanging down from their upper jaw. Baleen looks like a comb and feels a lot like our finger-nails. It helps the whales strain tiny plants and animals, called *plankton,* from the water. Baleen whales are larger in size than toothed whales. Some of these whales live in families of three or four whales. They migrate as the seasons change. You would see two blowholes on the top of a baleen whale.

Write **Toothed** or **Baleen** to tell which kind of whale matches the description:

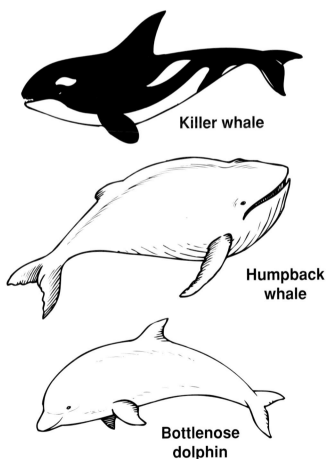

Killer whale

Humpback whale

Bottlenose dolphin

_____ has one blowhole

_____ lives in a family

_____ eats mostly plankton

_____ most do not migrate

_____ larger in size

_____ has two blowholes

_____ lives in a large group

_____ migrates

_____ eats fish

(Drawings not to scale.)

Note To The Teacher: Use with "What Is A Whale?" on page 28.

HOW BIG?!

Using a yardstick, measure the length of each whale.

Narwhal

Narwhal   _____   =   _____ ft.

Killer whale   _____   =   _____ ft.

Minke whale   _____   =   _____ ft.

Gray whale   _____   =   _____ ft.

Killer whale

Right whale   _____   =   _____ ft.

Bowhead whale _____   =   _____ ft.

Fin whale   _____   =   _____ ft.

Minke whale

Blue whale   _____   =   _____ ft.

Answer the questions using the whale lengths above.

Gray whale

1. Which whale is 45 feet long?

    _____

2. Which whale is larger than the bowhead whale but smaller than the blue whale?

    _____

Right whale

3. What is the difference in length between the killer whale and the right whale?

    _____

Bowhead whale

4. How long is the minke whale?

    _____

Fin whale

5. How many yardsticks would it take to equal the length of a narwhal?

Blue whale

    _____

Whale Migrations

Scientists study the travels of whales each spring and fall. The whales take the same routes every year. These regular whale journeys are called *migrations.* In the fall, humpback whales migrate to areas closer to the equator. In these warm waters, baby whales called *calves* are born. In late spring, whales travel back to the cold waters of the Arctic and Antarctic to feed.

Trace the humpback whales' fall migration routes.
Color each by the code:

1. From Alaska southeast to Baja California — blue
2. From Alaska south to Hawaii — red
3. From Iceland southwest to the Caribbean Sea — green
4. From Maine south to the Caribbean — yellow
5. From Antarctica north to Peru — orange
6. From Antarctica north to Brazil — purple

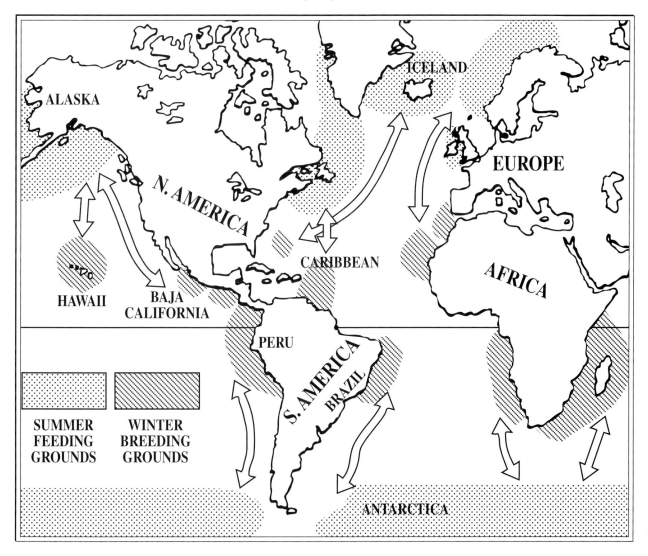

Those Wacky Whales
by

_____

Logging is when a group of whales rests on the surface, all facing the same direction. ⑤

Breaching is when a whale leaps out of the water headfirst, then falls back with a splash. ②

Sailing is when a whale raises its flukes high in the air and lets the wind carry it along. ⑥

Note To The Teacher: Use with "Those Wacky Whales" on page 35.

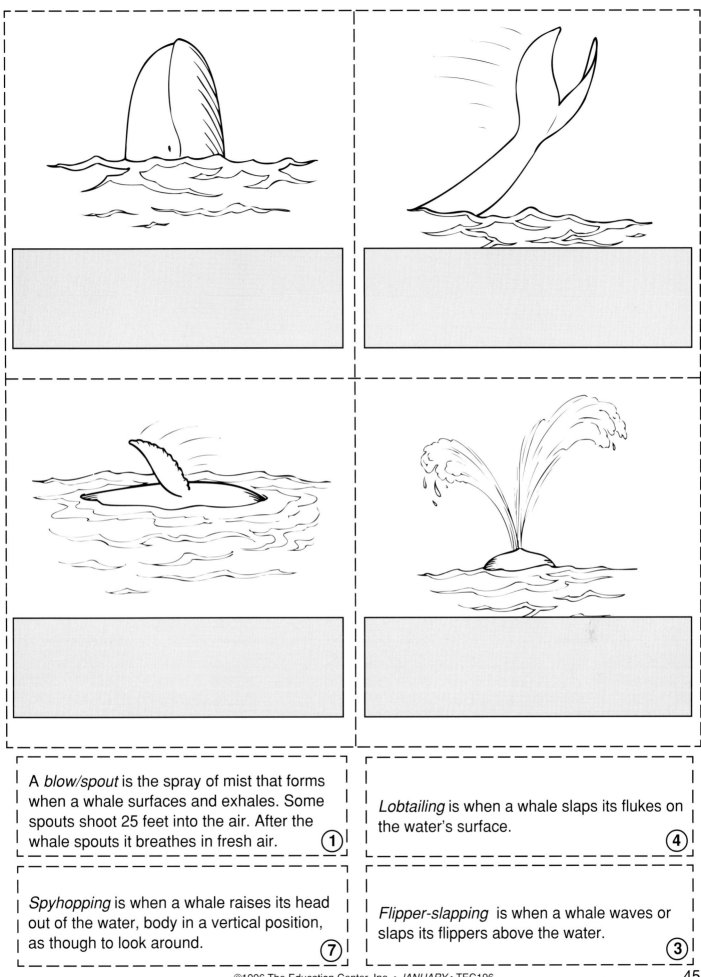

A *blow/spout* is the spray of mist that forms when a whale surfaces and exhales. Some spouts shoot 25 feet into the air. After the whale spouts it breathes in fresh air. ①

Spyhopping is when a whale raises its head out of the water, body in a vertical position, as though to look around. ⑦

Lobtailing is when a whale slaps its flukes on the water's surface. ④

Flipper-slapping is when a whale waves or slaps its flippers above the water. ③

Meet Bill Peet

Meet a literary star that your students are sure to take a shine to!
These Bill Peet books will soon become classroom favorites.

by Cynthia Holcomb

Welcome to the world of Bill Peet, where animals of all sorts and sizes are placed in situations with which young readers will easily identify. There are camels who feel inadequate, roosters who doubt their own abilities, trolls torn between good and bad decisions, gnats who are considered unimportant because of their size, and a host of other lovable characters!

Bill Peet has long been a favorite children's author and illustrator. He knew early on that he wanted to draw. He spent his school years secretly drawing in his schoolbooks! He also had a love for all living things. His childhood summers were spent out-of-doors, where he would organize "bring 'em back alive" safaris, capturing turtles, frogs, and minnows. His fascination with nature is very evident in his story lines.

It was during his time with Disney® that Peet began to work on children's literature. He now has over 30 titles to his credit and his books are read worldwide. He is also the author-illustrator of *Bill Peet: An Autobiography* (Houghton Mifflin Company, 1989). This Caldecott Honor book details his life from child to author.

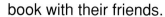

Amazing Animals

Before you begin your unit, let each student make a drawing of his favorite animal on a piece of white construction paper. Tell the students that their animals can have imaginative qualities and do not have to be completely realistic. Make sure that each student names his animal. After the students have heard a few of Bill Peet's stories, have them write adventures for their imaginary animals (see "All-Star Stories" below).

Front-Page News

When your students have become familiar with several of Bill Peet's books, let each child choose one of the stories to display on a newsworthy bulletin board. Make a copy of the Front-Page News pattern on page 50 for each student. Instruct students to complete their newspaper articles by writing details from the stories they have chosen. Display the finished projects on a newspaper-covered bulletin board. Add the title "Big News About Bill Peet!" Your class will enjoy spreading the news of a good book with their friends.

All-Star Stories

After reading aloud each Bill Peet story, give every student a copy of the reproducible "All-Star Story Map" on page 49. Direct students to think of the characters, setting, problem, and solution of a story. Show them where to write this information on their story maps. After you have shared a few stories with them, students will be eager to complete a map by themselves. As your students become well-acquainted with mapping out a story, they can use the outline for prewriting ideas when planning their own animal adventure stories.

Cock-A-Doodle Dudley

(Houghton Mifflin Company, 1990)

Dudley the rooster is one of the most popular animals on the farm. Although he is rather scrawny, his crowing ability is the talk of the barnyard. Even the sun, old Sol, favors Dudley's crowing above any other rooster's. Only one animal, a mean-spirited goose, is not a fan of Dudley's and sets out to cause problems for the rooster. The goose comes close to succeeding, but ends up causing problems for himself instead.

Some of the dangers that Dudley faces are due to the fact that he is a link in the *food chain.* He is in danger of being eaten by a fox and then an owl. Dudley does some eating too—he feasts on dragonflies, snails, and caterpillars. Point out to your students that old Sol plays a very important part in the food chain, since all plant growth depends on the sun. Without plants, the plant eaters couldn't survive. Without the plant eaters, the meat eaters would die out.

Your students can create a paper chain that is also a food chain. For each student, prepare four or five 1" x 8" paper strips with the names of some of the plants and animals from the story written on them. Tell the students to connect the paper strips in order from prey to predator (grass, snail, rooster, fox, etc.).

The Gnats Of Knotty Pine

(Houghton Mifflin Company, 1975)

The start of hunting season causes a panic for the forest animals, and a meeting is called to discuss a way to protect themselves from the hunters. Not one animal can come up with a plan—except for a tiny gnat named Nate. What was the gnat's idea? The animals never find out because they won't bother to listen to Nate. They rudely dismiss the gnat as bothersome and insignificant. When the hunters show up the next day, Nate and the other gnats forge ahead with their plan, causing the hunters to make a hasty retreat! The forest animals quickly change their minds about the insects.

The forest animals had a preconceived idea about the gnats—as pests! Discover what preconceived notions your students have about these animals: fox, deer, bee, bear, rabbit, skunk, owl, mouse, and pig. Have them supply adjectives to complete phrases such as "wise as an owl" or "sly as a fox."

Record their answers on chart paper or on construction-paper cutouts in the shape of each animal. After the students have heard the story, they may have changed their views on some of the animals!

Pamela Camel

(Houghton Mifflin Company, 1984)

After a life in the circus where she was called dumb, stupid, and bad-tempered, Pamela decides to run away. On her way across the country, she saves an express train from derailing on a broken track. Pamela finds that although she had not been a circus star, she is considered extraordinary by the people she helps.

Make the most of the many adjectives in this book to help students improve their descriptive writing. Create adjective word banks for overly used words. Label five charts with the words *good, bad, big, small,* and *nice.* Challenge students to find adjectives in the story to replace those words. Display the finished word banks in your classroom to remind students of the many word choices for use in their descriptive writing.

Jethro And Joel Were A Troll
(Houghton Mifflin Company, 1987)

A two-headed troll named Jethro and Joel lives quietly in the mountains. But one day, Joel decides to be more troll-like and stir up some trouble. Jethro reluctantly agrees to go along. (He has no choice—they share the same body!) The troll takes off through the countryside. Just as Joel's path of destruction reaches its peak, Jethro asserts his better judgment and finds that the troll can use a newfound talent to be helpful instead of harmful.

After reading the book, capitalize on the concept of opposites for vocabulary development. Ask students to imagine one body with two heads that are total opposites: Joel is fierce; Jethro is gentle. Joel likes trouble; Jethro wants peace. Can your class find words with opposite meanings? To make their own two-headed troll display that includes a list of antonyms, supply each student with two six-inch paper plates, a sheet of 12" x 18" construction paper, and pieces of craft paper in assorted colors and sizes. Demonstrate how to make the troll as shown.

After they complete their trolls, have the students brainstorm opposite words. When each student has thought of a pair, he writes them on his troll's body, one word of the pair on each side of the troll. Encourage students to find as many antonyms as possible. What a way to show off a vocabulary lesson!

Jennifer And Josephine
(Houghton Mifflin Company, 1967)

A junkyard cat and an old, abandoned auto find themselves taken from their peaceful back lot and on the wildest adventure of their lives. When Jennifer the auto is purchased by a traveling salesman, Josephine the cat hops into the backseat so that she will not be separated from her friend. The car's new owner is a dangerous and careless driver, and the friends find themselves on a most frightening trip. By sticking together, Jennifer and Josephine manage to survive. Safe but scared, the pair meet with a new owner and a happy ending.

Ask your students to predict what life will be like for Jennifer and Josephine with their new owner. What events could occur now that they live on a farm? Have each student write a story called "The Further Adventures Of Jennifer And Josephine." Allow each student to read his story to the class for an action-packed storytelling session.

good nice pretty day
bad mean ugly night

Other Titles By Bill Peet:
Big Bad Bruce (Houghton Mifflin Company, 1987)
Buford, The Little Bighorn (Houughton Mifflin Company, 1985)
Encore For Eleanor (Houghton Mifflin Company, 1985)
Huge Harold (Houghton Mifflin Company, 1982)
The Spooky Tail Of Prewitt Peacock (Houghton Mifflin Company, 1979)
Whingdingdilly (Houghton Mifflin Company, 1982)
The Wump World (Houghton Mifflin Company, 1991)

Name _____

All-Star Story Map

Characters

Setting

by

Name Of Book

Problem

Solution

Note To The Teacher: Use with "All-Star Stories" on page 46.

★★★ The Daily Star ★★★
Bill Peet Is An All-Star Author!

by _____

Bill Peet is making front-page news with his book

_____

My favorite character in the book is	The part of the story I like best is
_____	_____
because _____	_____
_____	_____
_____	_____
_____	_____
_____	_____
_____	_____
_____	_____
_____	_____
_____	_____
_____	_____
_____	_____
_____	_____
_____	_____

I think _____ would enjoy this book.

Note To The Teacher: Use with "Front-Page News" on page 46.

Meet Some Polar Pals

Plan a class expedition to the poles to discover how people and animals survive in the extremely cold temperatures of the Arctic and Antarctic. On your journey, students will learn about arctic habitats and polar animals while practicing basic skills.

ideas by Nancy Matthews and Kathy Wolf

This Place Is Cold!

Begin your study of arctic habitats with a geography lesson. To create some arctic excitement, pack your bags for an imaginary expedition to Alaska! Dress in a parka and boots, and bring along a backpack with items such as mittens, a flashlight, a stuffed toy polar bear, a book about Alaska, a map showing the Arctic, and a class supply of Eskimo Pies® or Polar Bars® for energy. Unpack your backpack and ask students if they can guess your destination. When students have guessed correctly, pull down a world map to pinpoint some polar places. Provide a copy of the map on page 60, and have students locate and color Alaska, the Arctic Circle, and Greenland.

Next pass out the Polar Bar® provisions for students to munch as you read aloud *This Place Is Cold* by Vicki Cobb (Walker and Company, 1989). After reading, let students share some of the fascinating facts they learned from the book. Then have students name arctic plants and animals and list these on a chart like the one shown. Post the chart where students can add additional arctic vocabulary words over the course of this unit. Use the chart as a reference for creative writing about polar pals.

animal	plant
lemming	reindeer moss
musk ox	blueberries
caribou	lichens
polar bear	algae
snowy owl	poppies
arctic tern	bluebells
arctic hare	
walrus	
seal	
reindeer	
arctic fox	
sled dog	
arctic wolf	

Frigid Facts To Share

- In Alaska, temperatures can drop to lower than 50 degrees below zero.
- People's breath turns to ice crystals, and their eyelashes, eyebrows, and skin can freeze if they are outside for only a few minutes.
- To keep car engines from freezing, people plug their cars into electrical outlets that keep engine-block heaters running.
- Frozen firewood can shatter with a tap from an ax.
- At very cold temperatures, snow makes a squeaking noise when people walk on it.
- In some places the frozen ground, or *permafrost,* does not thaw, even in the summer. Homes built on this land may sink as the heat from the houses causes the ice to melt and the ground shifts. People jack up crooked floors and doorways.
- Bush pilots bring food, medicine, and mail to remote settlements. In Alaska, one out of every 45 people has a pilot's license.

Grab Your Parkas!

How do animals and humans protect themselves from cold temperatures that can drop to lower than 50 degrees below zero? Point out to students that some animals—such as caribou, whales, and arctic terns—migrate to warmer locations for the winter months. Most arctic mammals, like musk oxen and polar bears, have thick hair to hold heat next to their bodies. Since whales and seals have little or no hair, they have thick layers of blubber to keep them warm in the cold ocean temperatures. Whale blubber can be up to 20 inches thick!

For centuries, native people have used the skins and furs of seals, bears, wolves, and caribou to make protective clothing. The clothes are loose-fitting to keep warm air between the layers. The seams are sewn tightly to make them waterproof. Have students look in magazines and catalogs for pictures of clothes that provide insulation, then cut out examples of this cold-weather clothing. Students paste these pictures on a poster to make a collage.

For a follow-up activity, divide your class into two teams for a cold-weather clothing relay. Provide a box with a hat, a muffler, and a pair of mittens for each team. Place these boxes behind a goal line. At a signal one player from each team races to the line and dons the apparel. The runner races back to his team, where he takes off the items and sits down. The next runner in line bundles up, runs back to the team's box, and takes off the clothing items, replacing them in the box. Then he runs back to his team and sits down. Continue in the same manner until all players have run and are sitting down.

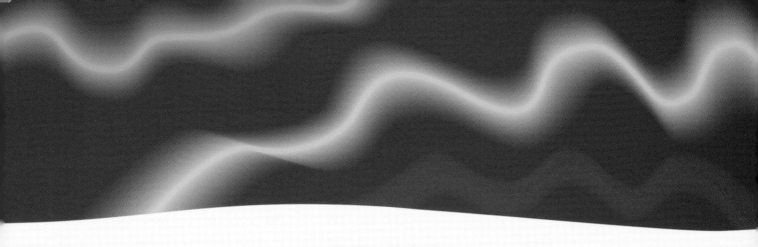

Northern Lights

Introduce the concept of long arctic nights and short winter days; then create an *aurora borealis* for a bulletin-board display. Demonstrate how the North Pole points away from the sun in winter with a classroom globe or a basketball to represent the earth. Mark the Arctic Circle with masking tape. Using a flashlight to represent the sun, tilt the earth away from the source of light and shine the light on the earth. Have a student use a piece of chalk to mark where the sun is shining directly. Tell students that—just south of the Arctic Circle—the sun comes up around lunchtime and stays up for just a few hours in the winter. Sometimes during arctic nights, the sky looks like a light show of swirling colored lights. This is called the *aurora borealis* or *northern lights*. In the Antarctic this phenomenon is known as the *aurora australis* or *southern lights*.

Display pictures of this phenomenon, if possible. Point out the North Pole and the South Pole on the globe, and explain that these colored lights are the result of solar particles in the atmosphere that are attracted to the earth's magnetic field at each pole. These particles make other small particles in our atmosphere move and seem to dance in the sky above the poles.

To create a classroom northern lights display, cover your bulletin board with dark blue or purple background paper. Cut out and mount white paper to represent snow along the bottom of the board. Provide students with colored chalk, and have them draw swirls of color in the sky. With a chalkboard eraser, wipe the colors in a downward motion. Blend these curtains of colors just to the horizon. Add a soft, orange sun low in the sky. Have students color and cut out polar animals, Inuit natives, and sled dogs to add to the board with the title "Northern Night-Lights."

Arctic Encounters

Continue your arctic adventure by reading aloud *Little Polar Bear* by Hans de Beer (Scholastic Inc., 1987); then create some cool habitat mobiles. In the story, Lars, a polar bear cub, drifts off to the tropics on an iceberg. He meets many new friends, all native to the tropics, while trying to find his way back home to the Arctic. After sharing the story, discuss some of the differences and similarities between arctic and tropical regions of the world such as the following:

- Both areas are home to water animals.
- Whales migrate from arctic waters to tropical waters, where their babies are born.
- Icebergs often break off from the polar ice floes and float with the currents for hundreds of miles before melting.

Compare and contrast the climates, landforms, and inhabitants of the Arctic and the tropics with a Venn diagram.

Reinforce this lesson by having students construct mobiles that represent the two regions. Provide each student with a paper plate, white construction paper, scissors, tape, yarn, and crayons. Tell each student to illustrate either a polar or a tropical scene on his paper plate. Tell the student to choose three animals from that region to illustrate on the construction paper and cut out. Provide a hole puncher for each student to punch three holes along the bottom of his paper plate as shown. The student tapes a length of yarn to the back of each animal cutout and ties the other end of each length through a hole in his plate. Have students hang their mobiles at home as reminders of the book, *Little Polar Bear*.

Jumbo Polar Trading Cards

To encourage research on arctic animals, have students create trading cards. Bring in samples of sports trading cards for students to examine; then discuss the kinds of information printed on them. Decide as a class what kinds of information would be important to know about an animal of the polar regions. (Facts such as size, polar region, habitat, food, camouflage, reproduction, and the number of young are a few examples.) List this information on the board.

To make oversized polar trading cards, distribute blank 5" x 7" cards. Each student chooses an arctic or antarctic animal and designs a trading card for his animal. On the front of his card, the student illustrates the animal in its habitat. On the reverse side, the student lists at least three important facts about the animal. Laminate the cards, cut them out, and put them in a central location for all students to read and study to brush up on their polar animal pals.

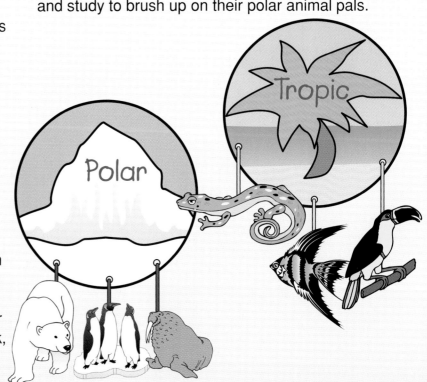

Polar-Bear Badges

Stuffed-toy polar bears look cute and cuddly, but real adult male polar bears can measure from 8 to 11 feet long and weigh more than 1,000 pounds! To visualize the size of an adult male polar bear, assist students in measuring and cutting ten feet of string. Then tape it along a wall for reference. Compare the weight of one polar bear to ten very petite teachers! Share the following information and help students pinpoint the locations of polar bears on a world map:

- Polar bears live along the northern coasts of Canada, Greenland, and the former Soviet Union, and near the northern coast of Alaska, as well as on islands in the Arctic Ocean.
- Polar bears eat seals, seabirds, lemmings, fish, grass, and berries. They can smell food as much as ten miles away.
- Polar bears are excellent swimmers and can also run up to 35 miles per hour for short distances.

Explain that polar bears were once killed by hunters for their valuable furs, until they were in danger of extinction. Today the United States, Canada, and other nations have laws to protect polar bears from hunting.

Students can show their support for the protection of polar bears by making and wearing their own "Friends Of The Polar Bear" badges. Provide a copy of the badge patterns on page 61 for each child to fill in, color, and cut out. Also provide each child with a 24-inch piece of yarn to glue between the two circles as shown. Encourage students to wear their badges around their necks and to share the information about these polar pals with their families.

Polar Bear Facts

Size: 8 to 11 feet
Appearance: white fur, big paws and claws, sharp teeth
Regions: Greenland, Canada, Alaska

Friends Of The Polar Bear

Todd James

Save The Seals

Share the following facts about seals. Then have students create posters and march to save the seals.

- Seals are terrific swimmers.
- Most seals live in groups and stay together for long ocean migrations. Ross seals of the Antarctic live alone or in pairs.
- Northern fur seals stay at sea for eight months, but their seal pups are born on land.
- Every spring the northern fur seals go to large beach areas, called *rookeries,* where their pups are born. More than 150,000 seals may gather at a rookery. The males or *bulls* arrive first and fight for territories on the beach. It's a noisy place with seals bellowing and roaring.
- A female seal is called a *cow.* She usually gives birth to only one pup. She can tell her baby from all the others by its cry and smell.
- The northern fur seal pup is black. These seal pups can swim as soon as they are born.
- Harp seal pups are born with soft, white fur, which they shed within one month.
- For hundreds of years, native people have hunted seals for blubber, bones, fur, and meat.

Provide pictures of different kinds of seals, including the newborn harp seal or *whitecoat.* Ask students to brainstorm why these animals might have been hunted almost to extinction. Then explain that during the 1800s, soft, silky seal fur was prized by commercial fur traders for making coats and hats. The fur trade almost made some species of seals extinct. In 1911 the United States, Canada, Russia, and Japan signed an agreement to only hunt northern fur seals on land. The yearly hunting harvest of newborn harp seals off Newfoundland was ended in 1985 due in part to the protests of animal rights activists.

Ask students to think of ways that they might help seals or other animals that are being killed for their furs. Provide poster board and paint sticks from a local building-supply store to make posters to promote awareness of the need for protection of seals. Encourage students to carry the posters in a Save The Seals parade.

Wally-The-Walrus Puppets

The walrus is classified as a type of large seal—the only seal with tusks. Walrus tusks are actually canine teeth that point downward and can grow to as long as 39 inches! To introduce this polar giant, pull out a yardstick and ask students to imagine teeth that long. Display photos of walruses and ask students to think of uses for such huge canine teeth. Then share the following information:

- Walruses have a unique food-gathering technique. They stand on their heads in the cold, arctic waters and use their long, sturdy tusks to scrape mollusks, sea urchins, and starfish from the ocean bottom. Their favorite food is clams.
- Walruses can defend themselves from polar bears or human hunters with their tusks.
- Walruses also use their tusks as hooks to pull themselves out of the water and onto the ice.
- The bristles on a walrus's upper lip are sensitive to touch and help the walrus find food.
- Adult walrus males can grow to about 12 feet long and weigh up to 3,000 pounds.
- The native Inuit people hunt walruses for meat. They used the hides to make shelters and boats and burned oil from walrus blubber for heat and light.

To visualize the size of an adult male walrus, help students measure and cut 12 feet of string; then tape it to the wall below the polar-bear string measurement and compare lengths. Students can compare the weight of an adult walrus to that of a small compact car.

Then, to reinforce what they have learned, have students create paper-bag puppets. Duplicate a class supply of the patterns on page 62 on white construction paper. Distribute a brown paper lunch bag and a copy of the patterns to each student. Provide scissors, glue, craft sticks, and crayons. Each student colors, cuts out, and glues his walrus patterns to the bag as shown. Have him color and cut out, then glue the clam and starfish cutouts to craft sticks. Allow student pairs to use their puppets to create a conversation between two walruses diving for food. Clam dip, anyone?

Sled-Dog Smart

For many years, sled dogs have been working dogs for people in the Far North. These hardy working dogs have been used for hunting, transportation, exploration, protection, law enforcement, and mail delivery. They have also been faithful friends and companions. In the early 1900s, sled dogs led the way for explorers to reach the North Pole and the South Pole. From 1873 to 1969, sled dog teams were used by Canada's mounted police to patrol the frontier. Sled dog teams also delivered mail to remote settlements in Alaska and Canada. Purebred sled dogs include the *Siberian husky,* the *Alaskan malamute,* the *Samoyed,* and the *Eskimo dog.* Mixed breeds are also used as sled dogs in the United States and Canada.

To introduce students to the importance of dogsledding, read *Susan Butcher And The Iditarod Trail* by Ellen M. Dolan (Walker and Company, 1993) or *The Bravest Dog Ever: The True Story Of Balto* by Natalie Standiford (Random House Books For Young Readers, 1989). Then have students create and name sled dogs of their own. Provide each child with a paper plate, scissors, glue, yarn, markers, felt or construction-paper scraps, two buttons or wiggle eyes, and a black pompom. Duplicate the dog face on page 64 for each student to color and cut out. Have each child glue the dog face to his paper plate. The child cuts out ears and a mouth from the felt or paper and glues them to the paper plate. Next he glues on the buttons or wiggle eyes and the pom-pom nose. Then demonstrate how to cut and glue pieces of yarn three to four inches in length as shown. When the projects have been completed, ask students to name their sled dogs and display them in cooperative teams.

To follow up, provide some skills practice at a learning center. Duplicate the patterns on page 65, and cut out pairs of sleds and dogs. Program the cutouts for matching skills, such as contractions and words, math facts and answers, or vocabulary words and definitions. Store the pairs in a string-tie envelope with directions and an answer key. Have students match pairs and mush on to success!

Long-Distance Champions

Wow your students with the incredible journey of the arctic tern! These amazing birds travel between homes at both poles. The arctic tern spends about 2 1/2 months on the tundra near the Arctic Circle for the mating and hatching seasons. It then flies an incredible 9,000 miles to winter in the Antarctic and enjoy what is summer there.

Introduce the arctic tern to students for map-skills practice. Provide each student with a copy of the reproducible map on page 60. Let students use the maps to discuss and trace the migratory route of the arctic tern.

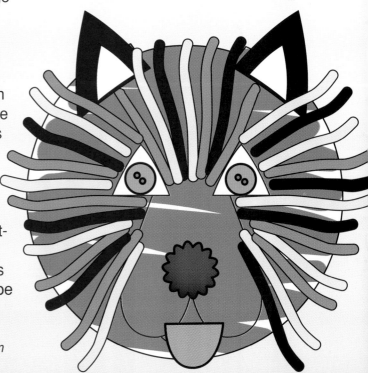

58   *idea contributed by Susan Willingham*

Arctic Tales

Share these books about the Arctic and Antarctic for some cool reading!

Where The Great Bear Watches

by James Sage
(USA Penguin Books Inc., 1993)
Share this story about an Inuit boy paddling in his kayak. After reading, ask students to recall the animals in the story. Discuss how the Inuit natives share the land, air, and water with arctic animals. Point out the polar bear tracks and have students make their own bear tracks appear in the snow with this art project. Provide each child with a piece of white paper and a white crayon. Have him draw bear tracks with the white crayon and then paint over the tracks with blue watercolor paint to create a crayon resist. Has a polar bear been by here?

White Bear, Ice Bear

by Joanne Ryder
(William Morrow & Company, Inc.; 1989)
This amusing story is about a boy who dreams of becoming a polar bear! On a cold, winter night, he sneaks out of his house for a moonlit adventure. After reading the story aloud, have each student write a similar story from the point of view of a polar bear and illustrate his adventures. Collect the stories and illustrations, and bind them into a class book titled "If I Were An Ice Bear…"

Arctic Spring

by Sue Vyner
(USA Penguin Books Inc., 1992)
The illustrations in this book point out that the Arctic can be a beautiful place in the spring. As you read aloud, discuss the animals' activities and ask students to guess why the polar bear is staying close to its den. Finish the story and ask if students were surprised by the ending. Did they anticipate the emergence of two cubs?

To follow up, have younger students pretend to be polar bear cubs emerging from their den. Ask them to tell what they would see in the arctic spring.

More Arctic Tales

Little Polar Bear And The Brave Little Hare by Hans de Beer (North-South Books, Inc.; 1992)
Life In The Polar Lands: Animals, People, Plants by Monica Byles (Scholastic Inc., 1993)
The Arctic Land by Bobbie Kalman (Crabtree Publishing Company, 1988)

Arctic Regions Of The World

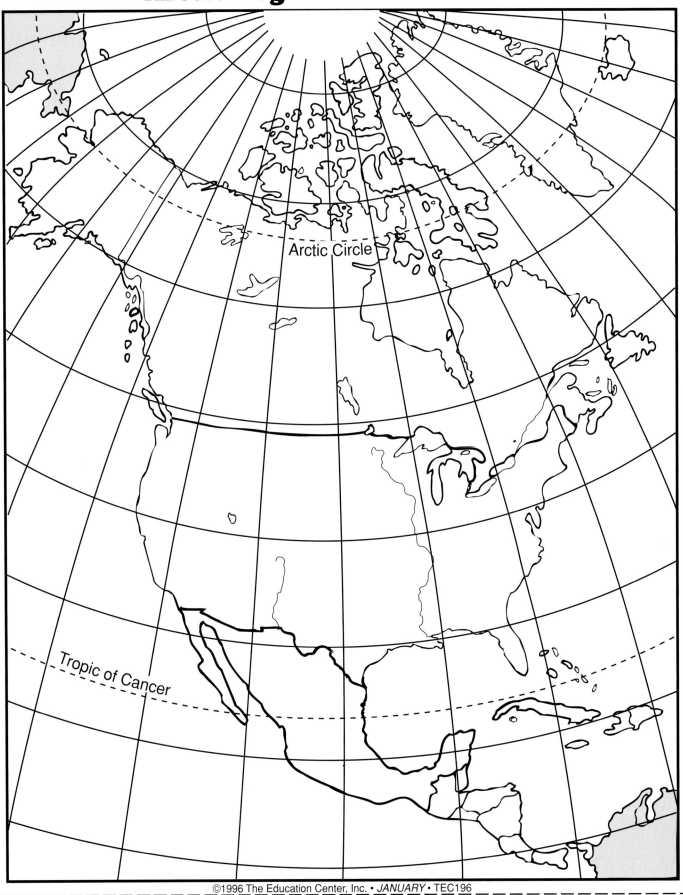

Arctic Circle

Tropic of Cancer

©1996 The Education Center, Inc. • *JANUARY* • TEC196

Note To The Teacher: Use with "This Place Is Cold!" on page 51 and "Long-Distance Champions" on page 58.

Friends Of The Polar Bear

Polar Bear Facts

Size:_____

Appearance:_____

_____

_____

Regions:_____

_____

Patterns

Use with "Wally-The-Walrus Puppets" on page 57.

Polar Pals

Read the clues and complete the puzzle.
Use the word bank to help you.

Across

3. I use my fluffy tail as a blanket on cold winter nights.
4. I dig for clams on the ocean floor with my tusks.
7. I am a bird that does not fly.
8. I have a thick, shaggy coat and curved horns.
10. It takes me months to fly from my home in the North to my home in the South.

Word Bank

lemming	musk ox
caribou	penguin
arctic fox	walrus
snowy owl	arctic hare
polar bear	
arctic tern	

Down

1. I am related to the reindeer.
2. I am an excellent swimmer and can smell food ten miles away.
5. My sensitive nose helps me find twigs under the snow in the winter.
6. I make tunnels in the tundra grass during the summer.
9. I can hunt at night with my keen eyesight.

Dog Face Patterns
Use with "Sled-Dog Smart" on page 58.

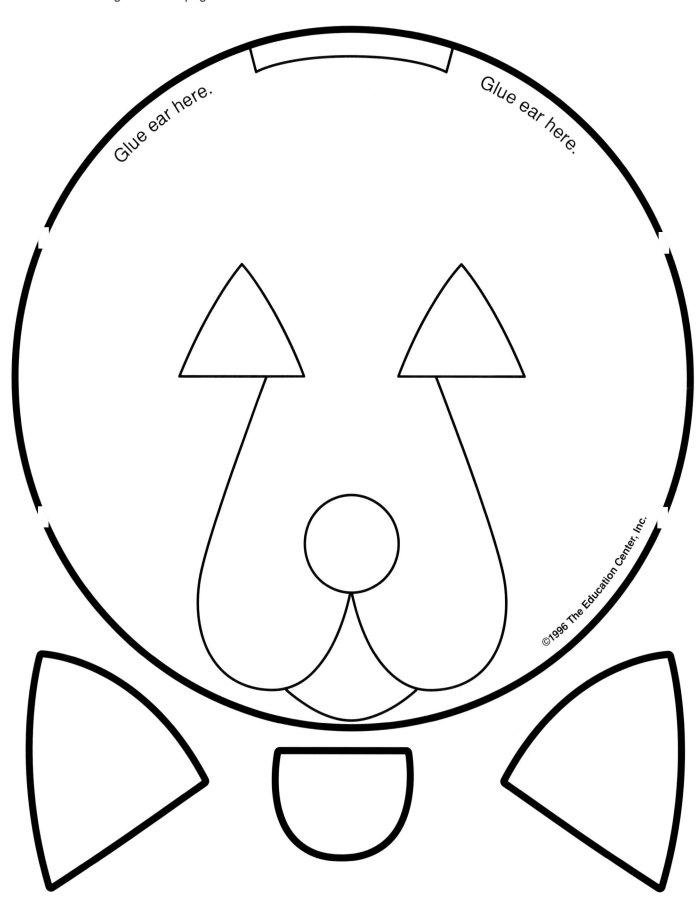

Glue ear here.

Glue ear here.

©1996 The Education Center, Inc.

A PARADE OF PENGUINS

Grab your parka and head for the Antarctic for a parade of perky penguin ideas! Urge your students to "chill out" with wintry, penguin-related literature and activities.

by Susie Kapaun and Susan Hohbach

PENGUIN PARTNERS

Introduce your students to penguins by reading the story *Solo* by Paul Geraghty (Crown Publishers, Inc.; 1995). The endearing main character, Solo, leads students on an Antarctic adventure. The story describes an amazing penguin quality—the ability to locate a chick or mate by recognizing its distinctive voice.

After reading, engage students in this selective listening activity. In advance gather a class supply of small index cards; then sort the cards into pairs. Program each pair of cards with the same animal, such as "cat," "lion," "dog," "frog," "sheep," etc. Combine all the prepared cards in a container. Have each student randomly choose a card from the container. Explain to the class that each student is to walk around the room and make the sound of the animal he has selected. When he finds a classmate making the same sound, he stops and waits quietly with his newfound partner. As groups form, the room becomes quiet and your students are sorted penguin-style for a partner activity of your choice.

FASCINATING PENGUIN FACTS

Fascinate your students by sharing these fabulous facts.
• Penguins are speedy swimmers—averaging speeds between four and six miles per hour.
• Penguins can stretch their mouths, throats, and stomachs to swallow their prey whole.
• Penguins are known to walk in lines—as if playing Follow The Leader.
• Penguins eat seafood such as fish, krill, and squid.
• The largest penguin—the emperor penguin—can be as tall as four feet high and may weigh up to 100 pounds.
• During the breeding season, penguins gather on land or ice in large colonies called *rookeries*.
• Penguins group together for protection while swimming, but most work alone while hunting.

PENGUINS ON PARADE

Students will line up to take part in this penguin painting project. Enlarge the penguin pattern on page 71 to fit on a 9" x 12" piece of paper. Duplicate one copy for each student on white construction paper. Provide the students with small containers of black paint and orange paint and cotton swabs. Using a cotton swab, each student dabs orange paint onto the penguin pattern—filling in the beak and feet areas only. Next have him use a second cotton swab to apply black paint onto the penguin's body and wings using the same technique. Emphasize that the stomach is left white. To present a pleasing array of penguins on parade, staple the finished penguins to a bulletin board in rows as shown.

DIVE INTO PENGUIN FACTS!

All penguins live in the Southern Hemisphere, but only seven species live on the shores of Antarctica—the *emperor, king, Adelie, gentoo, chinstrap, macaroni,* and *rockhopper.* Add a splash of excitement to researching penguin facts by having students create life-size penguins. Divide your class into seven groups and assign each group the name of one Antarctic species. Provide resource books or computer references, and have each group research facts about its penguin, determine the penguin's height, and find a picture showing its features and coloring. Supply each group with a piece of bulletin-board paper that will accommodate the size of its penguin. Have each group measure, draw, and color a life-size picture of its penguin. Then create a small poster stating the penguin's name and a short list of facts. Display the finished projects and posters in a hallway. The whole school will dive into penguin facts with this unconventional display!

PROGRAMMABLE PENGUINS

Emperor penguins lay and care for one egg at a time. Your students will enjoy matching these adult penguins with their eggs while practicing an important skill. Reproduce 10–15 copies of the penguin pattern from page 71 on white construction paper. Cut an equal number of egg shapes from white construction paper. Color the penguins and program them with contractions, math facts, or opposites. Print a matching answer on each egg. Place the penguins and eggs in a string-tie envelope with directions and an answer key to make a Penguin Pocket Pal. The penguins and eggs will generate lively conversations about penguins and teach valuable skills at the same time.

5
x 5

25

Directions:
1. Match each emperor penguin to his egg.
2. Check the answer key.

hot

cold

can not

can't

68

BRRRR!!!!!

Students will love reading their way through these chilly choices about penguins!

CINDERELLA PENGUIN OR THE LITTLE GLASS FLIPPER

by Janet Perlman
(Puffin Books, 1995)

Your students will love the transformation of this story. In a parody of the classic, *Cinderella,* this retelling portrays the characters as penguins instead of people. As a class, brainstorm other favorite fairy tales. Read original versions of these classics; then have students change the main characters to penguins. An example might be "Goldilocks Penguin And The Three Polar Bears."

Have students work in groups to write a new a version of their favorite tale. Bind the various stories and keep them in your classroom library. These funny fairy tales are sure to be among your students' favorites.

TACKY THE PENGUIN

by Helen Lester
(Houghton Mifflin Company, 1988)

Single out this activity to highlight each student's individuality! After reading this comical tale about Tacky, discuss how Tacky is unique. Emphasize that each person is special in his own way; then give each student a copy of the "Uniquely You!" form on page 71. Have each student read and answer the questions. At the bottom of his form, the student writes something unique about himself. The student may choose a special talent, an unusual place he has visited, or a description of a collection of which he is proud.

Collect the forms from the students and have all of them stand. Select one form to begin the activity. Choose a numbered item from the form and make a statement such as "Remain standing if your favorite pet is a cat," or "Continue to stand if baseball is your favorite sport." A student sits down if his answer does not fit the statement. Continue making statements in this manner until only one special student is left standing. Return the form to that student and have him read aloud what makes him unique. Draw a new form from those that are left and ask students to stand before you repeat this one-of-a-kind activity.

PERFECT PENGUIN PICKS!

Antarctica
by Helen Cowcher
(Scholastic Inc.,1990)

Cuddly Dudley
by Jez Alborough
(Scholastic Inc.,1993)

Little Penguin
by Patrick Benson
(Philomel Books, 1990)

Little Penguin's Tale
by Audrey Wood
(Scholastic Inc.,1989)

SOMETHING FISHY

Reel in your students with these tasty math activities that involve a favored food of penguins—fish. Provide each student with a mixture of fish-shaped crackers in a small cup. Include a variety such as cheddar, pretzel, plain, etc. Use these manipulatives to have your students net some number practice. Have each student:

- estimate the number of fish in her cup
- sort the fish and group them by type
- place each group of fish in a row on her desk to create a graph
- determine the fish types with the most and least
- determine what fraction of the fish are cheddar
- create a pattern with the various fish
- imagine that each fish has a value of five cents and solve to find the total value

Have students eat their catch after you hook them on math practice!

PENGUIN PARTICIPATION

Have students review some remarkable penguin features with these creative culminating activities. Share each unusual penguin fact below; then engage your students in the accompanying activity.

- **Fact:** Penguins can jump out of the water and land on their feet. The height reached in this leap may be three times the penguin's own.
- **Activity:** Measure the distance each student can leap after he takes a running start.

- **Fact:** Penguins frequently follow one another in straight lines.
- **Activity:** Involve students in a game of Follow The Leader.

- **Fact:** A male emperor penguin can move about with an egg balancing atop his feet.
- **Activity:** Have each student try to walk a distance while balancing a clay-filled plastic egg or a hard-boiled egg on his feet.

- **Fact:** Penguins' short legs cause them to waddle when they walk. Their flippers often stand out slightly because they can not bend.
- **Activity:** Have students model a penguin and compete in a relay race. In turn, each student waddles with a rubber ball between his knees and keeps his arms very stiff.

- **Fact:** When penguins dive for fish, they can hold their breaths for up to three minutes.
- **Activity:** Time each student while he completes a physical activity such as hopping, jumping rope, running, etc. Discover how many students can continue their activity for the entire three minutes.

Pattern
Use with "Penguins On Parade" on page 67.
Use with "Programmable Penguins" on page 68.

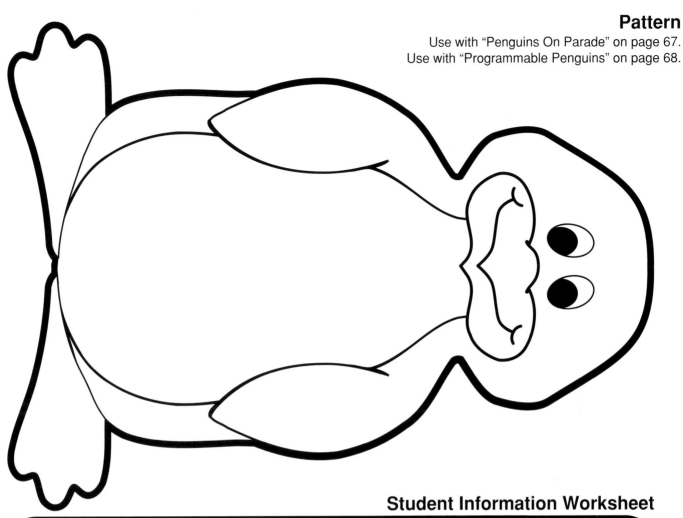

Student Information Worksheet

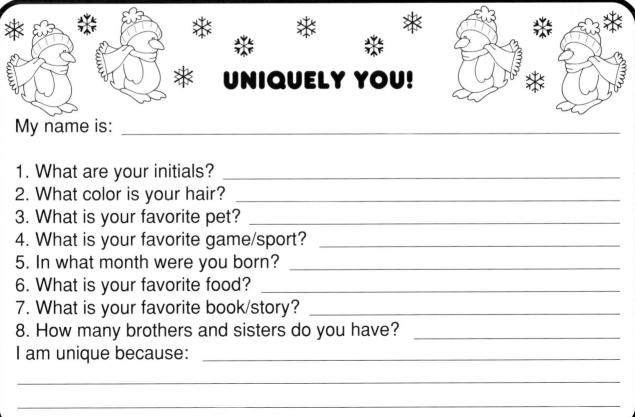

UNIQUELY YOU!

My name is: _____

1. What are your initials? _____
2. What color is your hair? _____
3. What is your favorite pet? _____
4. What is your favorite game/sport? _____
5. In what month were you born? _____
6. What is your favorite food? _____
7. What is your favorite book/story? _____
8. How many brothers and sisters do you have? _____
I am unique because: _____
_____
_____

Happy Birthday, Ben Franklin!

Benjamin Franklin was born on January 17, 1706. Introduce students to this American statesman, writer, printer, and inventor. Celebrate Ben's birthday to kick off a unit on inventors and their inventions.

ideas by Michel Gunther and Kathy Wolf

Franklin Inventions
bifocals
lighning rod
Franklin stove
glass harmonica
ng arm po

What's The Big Idea?

To introduce students to this famous American, read aloud *What's The Big Idea, Ben Franklin?* by Jean Fritz (Coward-McCann, Inc.; 1982) or *The Many Lives Of Benjamin Franklin* by Aliki (Simon & Schuster Books For Young Readers, 1988). Like many inventors, Ben Franklin was a curious person who conducted many experiments. His inventions include the lightning rod, a chair that turned into a ladder, the Franklin stove, and bifocals. After reading, make a list of Franklin's inventions on chart paper. Ask each student to choose one of Franklin's inventions and write why he thinks it was a good idea at the time and whether it would still be a good idea today.

Poor Richard

Ben Franklin was famous for printing a yearly calendar called *Poor Richard's Almanack.* It was full of information such as weather forecasts, tidal changes, astrology, news, recipes, cures for ailments, advice on when to plant and harvest, and of course, inventions! People bought the almanac especially for the witty sayings and advice from Poor Richard, a pseudonym for the author, Ben Franklin.

Provide a copy of a current almanac, if possible, for students to examine. Ask students to think about why people still consult almanacs today. Share some of Poor Richard's sayings and discuss their meanings. Write several of the sayings on a chart and select one each day for handwriting practice. Collect the sayings and have students compile them into individual booklets. Allow each student to create a cover for his handwriting sampler, as shown. Encourage students to take their almanacs home to share with their families.

Poor Richard's
anack

Poor
Tammy's
Almanac

Founding Father Of The Library

Another of Franklin's claims to fame is his creation of the first free public lending library. Arrange for your class to visit the school library and ask the librarian to share some books about Ben Franklin. Ask students why they think his idea of circulating books at no cost is still needed today. Ask them to tell what Franklin would say if he could see your library today. Challenge students to look around the library and find inventions that were unheard of in colonial times.

Back in your classroom, provide bulletin-board paper for students to create a banner to thank the founder of the public library system. Hang the banner in your school or public library in a place of honor.

HAPPY BIRTHDAY BENJAMIN FRANKLIN FOUNDER OF THE PUBLIC LIBRARY MRS. DECKER'S CLASS THANKS YOU!

Hods Bodkins!

To: Benjamin Franklin
From: Orville Wright

Benjamin Franklin Birthday Bash

Plan a birthday party for Ben with a guest list of notable inventors. Have each child choose a famous inventor from the list on page 78 and come to the party as that inventor with a gift-wrapped invention or representation of his invention. Provide gift tags for students to fill in as shown. Students attach the tags to their presents and come prepared to share facts about the inventor. Open the presents one at a time and have each child tell about his invention. Display the inventions with their gift tags on tables. Invite another classes to examine the loot from Ben's Birthday Bash. Serve Eskimo Pies®—invented by Christian Nelson in 1920!

More Books About Benjamin Franklin

Benjamin Franklin: A Man Of Many Jobs by Carol Greene (Childrens Press®, 1988)
Benjamin Franklin: Printer, Inventor, Statesman by David Adler (Holiday House, Inc.; 1992)

Why Didn't I Think Of That?

Begin your inventors unit by brainstorming a list of favorite inventions. Discuss how even ideas that are small in size can mean big changes in the way people work and play. Classify the list into two categories: big inventions and little inventions. Ask each student to choose one and tell how life would be different without it. Here are some to get you started:

Little Inventions	Big Inventions
Band-Aid®	television
soap	car
fork	computer
chocolate-chip cookies	airplane
umbrella	movies
paper clip	washing machine
lightbulb	microwave oven
rubber band	clothes dryer
Post-It™ Brand notes	telephone
LifeSavers®	

Post-It™ notes! Why didn't I think of that?!

get milk

Invention Pyramids

Emphasize that some inventions are the result of many people working together as a team or building on previous ideas. For example, the bicycle could not have been invented without the invention of the wheel. For an exercise in critical thinking, build some invention pyramids that demonstrate this concept.

Together, take a closer look at several inventions. Ask students to think of the ideas or materials that were needed in order for each invention to be completed. List these on the board, as shown, in pyramid fashion with the invention at the top. Then divide students into groups of three or four and provide 10–12 index cards for each group. Tell each group to choose an invention and build a pyramid by labeling the index cards. Help students mount their pyramids on a bulletin board. Provide additional cards so classmates may add to the invention pyramids as they discover new building blocks.

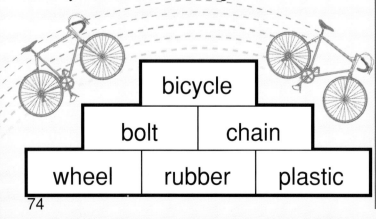

bicycle	
bolt	chain
wheel	rubber	plastic

The History Of An Invention

Have student groups create timelines to show how inventions have evolved over the years. Have each group choose one invention to research and draw a picture-sequence chart showing the changes. For example, timelines may show how Thomas Edison's electric lamp has evolved or what Alexander Graham Bell's telephone has looked like over the years. Automobiles, airplanes, household appliances, sports equipment, tools, and farm equipment are just a few of the inventions that have changed dramatically over the years. Have student groups share their picture timelines and display them by clipping the pictures in sequence on a line strung across the classroom or in the hall.

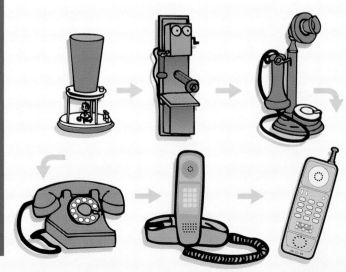

Inventors Hall Of Fame

Create an "Inventors Hall Of Fame" bulletin board to display student research about some great inventors. Duplicate the list on page 78 and have each student choose one of the inventions to research. Have him draw the invention or cut out a picture of it from a magazine or catalog. Provide each student with a 12" x 18" piece of white construction paper and have him glue his invention to it. Instruct the student to label it and write the inventor's name and the date the invention was developed. For an award-winning touch, have each child color and cut out the blue-ribbon patterns. Mount the pictures with the blue ribbons on a bulletin board with the title.

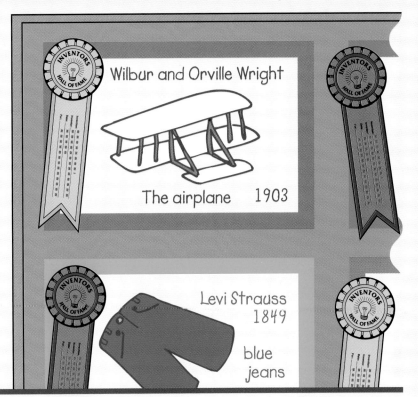

The Inventor's Notebook

Once students have had some background on inventions, they'll be ready to start thinking like inventors! These student-made booklets will help them formulate inventions of their own. Provide each student with a copy of the booklet pages on page 79 to cut out and assemble as shown.

Explain that many inventors kept notes on their experiments and jotted down their discoveries or thoughts for new products in notebooks. Ask students to think about how inventors came up with their ideas for inventions. (Share these examples: Louis Braille was blind and wanted to be able to enjoy books. Alexander Graham Bell was teaching deaf children. Benjamin Franklin wanted to make life easier, safer, and enjoyable.) Ask each student to think of a problem and an invention that would make life easier. Have him write his ideas in the space provided on page 2.

Once each student has identified a need, have him draw his invention and tell what it would do on page 3. On page 4, the student names his invention or gives it a trademark, special lettering, or spelling. Have each student add the letters ™ following his invention name to make it "official"!

On page 5, each student fills out a *patent*. Explain to students that a patent is a piece of paper that protects the inventor's idea. If an invention is patented, no one else can make it or sell it. Have students fill in the form with the date, inventor, and name of the invention; then stamp each page with an official-looking stamp or sticker.

On page 6, students plan how to advertise their inventions. To get started have students examine other advertisements for slogans or selling features. Then have each student draw an ad or write a slogan on this page. Place the completed notebooks in a shoebox at a center for all to read about some bright ideas.

The Invention Center

Provide your students with a hands-on exercise in creativity by setting up an invention center in a classroom corner. You'll have an industrial revolution on your hands! Enlist students' and parents' aid in collecting tissue, shoe, and cereal boxes; paper-towel tubes; margarine tubs; and other recyclable materials. Provide yarn, tape, paper scraps, and other project scraps. Allow students to visit the center in pairs or small cooperative groups to create inventions. Instruct each group to label a placard with the name of the invention, the inventors' names, and a brief description of the invention. To display the inventions, create a museum setting in your classroom or hallway. Set up tables for designated categories such as transportation, food, clothing, and communication. Have students place their inventions and descriptions in the correct category. Invite other classes to visit your classroom museum. Allow inventors to explain their creations in person or in tape-recorded museum messages.

Name That Invention!

For vocabulary development, write these inventions on the board and point out that many inventions have prefixes in their names:

- automobile
- audiotape
- aquarium
- bifocals
- microwave
- megaphone
- telephone

Have students use dictionaries to find the meanings of the prefixes and to write examples of other inventions that use prefixes. Challenge students to use prefixes in the names of the inventions they create at the invention center.

bifocals....
hmmm...

Advertising The Product

Some inventors, like Ben Franklin, do not want money for their inventions, but prefer to share their ideas with the world. Most inventors, however, want to sell their ideas. Companies want people to buy their new products. For a lesson on consumer education, ask each student to find an advertisement for a new product. Have old magazines, circulars, and newspaper ads on hand for students to search through. Ask students to examine the ads and look for words, logos, or pictures that the advertisers use to get the readers' attention. Ask, "Does this ad promise the buyer something? Is the product shown actual size?"

Point out that many inventors seek patents for their products. Explain that patents are given by the government to establish who owns the invention and who can make money from the idea. A product name may also have a trademark which reserves the right to use a certain name or spelling. Have students look for examples of ® or ™ on brand names and cut these out. Allow students to share their findings with the class. Glue the cutouts on a large piece of poster board to create a trademark collage. Encourage each student to design a personal trademark or logo to use on his personal property, notebooks, or assignments. Display student-brand good work for all to admire!

Miracle of the age!

GET ONE NOW!

OPERATERS ARE STANDING BY!

SUPPLIES ARE LIMITED

Three Inventors

Cut each sentence strip below, and match it to the inventor.
Glue it in the space under the inventor's name.

THREE INVENTORS

Thomas Alva Edison

Alexander Graham Bell

Marie Curie

Patented 1,000 inventions!

Created the first telephone in 1876.

Made discoveries that have helped fight cancer.

Invented the phonograph in 1877 and the electric light in 1880.

The world's first great woman scientist.

Taught deaf children.

Inventors Hall of Fame

Circle one invention to research.
Fill in the award below.
Color, cut out, and assemble the award.
Display the award with a picture of the invention.

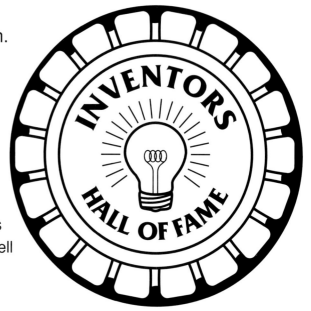

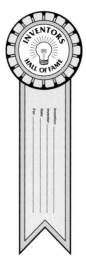

printing type	1438	Johann Gutenberg
thermometer	1593	Galileo Galilei
bicycle	1839	Kirkpatrick Macmillan
sewing machine	1846	Elias Howe
blue jeans	1849	Levi Strauss
dynamite	1866	Alfred Nobel
typewriter	1873	Christopher L. Sholes
telephone	1876	Alexander Graham Bell
electric lamp	1878	Thomas Alva Edison
gas-powered car	1885	Karl Benz
box camera	1888	George Eastman
zipper	1893	Whitcomb Judson
radio	1894	Guglielmo Marconi
cornflakes	1894	John H. Kellogg
Frisbee®	1900	Joseph P. Frisbie
airplane	1903	Wilbur and Orville Wright
Keds® sneakers	1917	Henry McKinney
television	1923	John L. Baird
liquid fuel rocket	1926	Robert Goddard
jet engine	1937	Frank Whittle
ballpoint pen	1940	Laszlo Biro
Polaroid camera	1947	Edwin Land

Invention: _____

Inventor: _____

Date: _____

Awarded by: _____

Note To The Teacher: Use with "Benjamin Franklin Birthday Bash" on page 73 and "Inventors Hall Of Fame" on page 75.

THE INVENTOR'S NOTEBOOK

_____
(name)

©1996 The Education Center, Inc.

1

Inventor's Notes

A job that is hard for me is:

_____

_____

I wish I could travel by:

_____

_____

I wish I could play a game that:

_____

_____

2

I would like to invent:
(describe it or draw a picture)

My invention would:

_____

_____

_____

3

The trademark for my invention
would be:

4

THE PATENT

On this _____ day of _____,
a letter of patent is issued to

_____,
for the invention of _____.
This letter of patent excludes others from
making, using, or selling this invention
throughout the United States of America.

5

My Advertisement

6

DISTINCTLY DINOSAURS

Are you ready to dig into a unit on dinosaurs? Get off to a colossal start by sharing a book that will spark student interest and creative thinking!
ideas by Kelly O'Connor and Cynthia Holcomb

Imagine That!

Can I Have A Stegosaurus, Mom? Can I!? Please? (written by Lois G. Grambling, Bridgewater Books, 1995) tells of a child who considers all the possibilities of having a stegosaurus as a pet. After reading, discuss what might happen if a student really did try to keep a dinosaur. How many of the students in your class *would* like a dinosaur for a pet? Have each student write a story telling what could happen if he brought a dinosaur home with him. Allow the students to illustrate their stories and share them with the class. The stage will be set for a "dino-mite" learning adventure!

Really Reptiles

Lead your students to the facts about these big creatures by starting out with a lesson on reptiles. Inform your students that each animal in the reptile family is cold-blooded, is covered with scaly skin or plates, breathes with lungs, and has a backbone. Display pictures of modern-day reptiles such as turtles, lizards, and crocodiles, and compare them with pictures of dinosaurs. (Magazines such as *Zoobooks*® and *Ranger Rick*®, and *The Big Book Of Dinosaurs* by Angela Wilkes [Dorling Kindersley Publishing, 1994] will provide you with some excellent illustrations.) Have students observe similarities between the two sets of pictures such as scaly skin, tails, location of eyes, etc. Record their observations. Ask the children to surmise why dinosaurs are included in the reptile family.

"Eggs-act" Facts

Another reptilian trait exhibited by dinosaurs was egg-laying. Many dinosaurs had nests that held their eggs until they hatched. How big do your students think a dinosaur egg might have been? They may be surprised that medium-sized dinosaurs laid eggs that were about the size of chicken or turkey eggs. The largest dinosaur eggs were about ten inches long. If they had been any larger, the weight of the baby would have cracked or broken the shell.

Read *Dinosaur Babies* by Maida Silverman (Simon and Schuster Children's Books, 1988) for more information about these egg-laying reptiles. Have students make a nest of dinosaur facts by filling a straw basket with eggs containing information from the story. Each student will need two or three plastic eggs and a few strips of paper. (Post-It™ notes or dinosaur-shaped notepad pages work well.) Instruct the students to write a fact on each piece of paper and place one fact in each plastic egg. Collect the eggs in the straw basket and allow students to take turns opening an egg and reading the fact inside. Your students will want to add more eggs to the nest as they learn more and more about dinosaurs!

Prehistoric Pairs

Use the patterns on pages 90 and 91 to create a game that will familiarize students with the different types of dinosaurs. Make a copy of each page; then cut out the pictures of the dinosaurs and glue the pictures and the names on separate index cards.

To play the game, have students arrange all the pictures and the names facedown on a table. Each student takes a turn by selecting two cards and turning them faceup. If the name matches the picture, the student will pick up the cards and take another turn. If the name does not match the picture, the student replaces the cards and the next player takes a turn, continuing until all the pairs have been matched. The student holding the most pairs is the "Match-a-saurus" and the winner of the game!

Pentaceratops
(pen-ta-ser-a-tops)

Tyrannosaurus rex
(tie-ran-oh-saw-rus recks)

Stegosaurus
(steg-o-saw-rus)

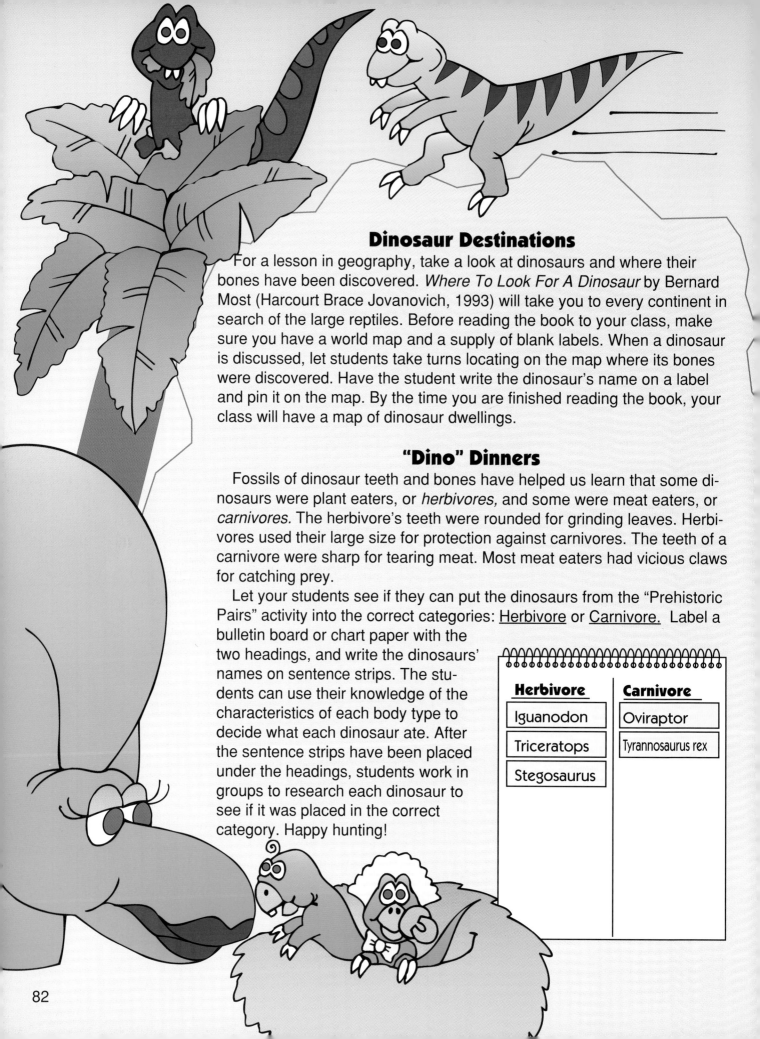

Dinosaur Destinations

For a lesson in geography, take a look at dinosaurs and where their bones have been discovered. *Where To Look For A Dinosaur* by Bernard Most (Harcourt Brace Jovanovich, 1993) will take you to every continent in search of the large reptiles. Before reading the book to your class, make sure you have a world map and a supply of blank labels. When a dinosaur is discussed, let students take turns locating on the map where its bones were discovered. Have the student write the dinosaur's name on a label and pin it on the map. By the time you are finished reading the book, your class will have a map of dinosaur dwellings.

"Dino" Dinners

Fossils of dinosaur teeth and bones have helped us learn that some dinosaurs were plant eaters, or *herbivores,* and some were meat eaters, or *carnivores.* The herbivore's teeth were rounded for grinding leaves. Herbivores used their large size for protection against carnivores. The teeth of a carnivore were sharp for tearing meat. Most meat eaters had vicious claws for catching prey.

Let your students see if they can put the dinosaurs from the "Prehistoric Pairs" activity into the correct categories: Herbivore or Carnivore. Label a bulletin board or chart paper with the two headings, and write the dinosaurs' names on sentence strips. The students can use their knowledge of the characteristics of each body type to decide what each dinosaur ate. After the sentence strips have been placed under the headings, students work in groups to research each dinosaur to see if it was placed in the correct category. Happy hunting!

Herbivore	Carnivore
Iguanodon	Oviraptor
Triceratops	Tyrannosaurus rex
Stegosaurus	

Brontosaurus 88 ft.

Triceratops 30 ft.

Deinonychus 10 ft.

How Big Was Big?

For a look at some super sizes, read *How Big Were The Dinosaurs?* by Bernard Most (Harcourt Brace & Company, 1994). This book compares dinosaurs to familiar objects. To get a realistic picture of dinosaur sizes, take your class into the hallway with some tape, string, and a measuring stick. Allow the children to measure the estimated lengths of some of the dinosaurs they have been studying. Tape one end of the string at the starting point and unwind the string until you have the length of the dinosaur marked off; then tape that end as well. Be sure to label each string with the dinosaur's name, picture, and length. A display of this size will be sure to grab the attention of anyone walking down the hallway!

Extend this activity with an exercise in graphing. Use the reproducible "How Big Were They?" on page 89 to record the lengths of these large reptiles. When students have completed the graph, they will know— when it comes to size, dinosaurs really measured up!

Tracking Down Similes

Display student writing in a big way! To prepare, duplicate the pattern on page 88 on brown or green paper. Have the class practice using similes to describe things in the classroom (the globe is as round as a basketball, the rug is as blue as the sky, etc.) When the students have caught on to the idea, let them each choose a dinosaur to describe. Ask, "How big was an apatosaurus? How fierce was a tyrannosaurus?" When they are ready to write their dinosaur similes, distribute the dinosaur-track patterns. Students can write their similes, cut out the patterns, and watch as the classroom bulletin board becomes covered with very descriptive tracks!

Our Dinosaur Display

"Dinos" On Display

For this interactive bulletin board, have students put their artistic abilities and research skills to work. Each student will need two pieces of white drawing paper. On one sheet, have each student make a drawing of one of the dinosaurs that he has learned about. On the other piece of paper, have him make a fact sheet about the dinosaur. When both papers are finished, staple them to the bulletin board so that the drawing is on top and the fact sheet is behind it. Students will enjoy admiring the drawings and lifting the flaps to see if they have correctly identified each dinosaur.

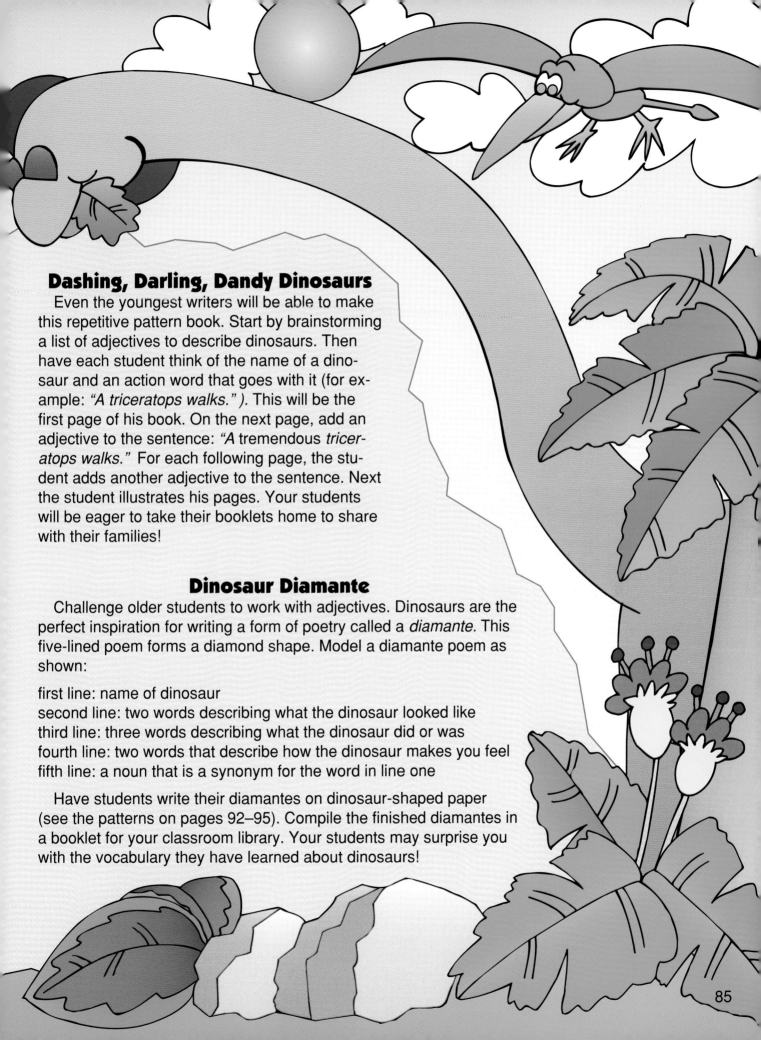

Dashing, Darling, Dandy Dinosaurs

Even the youngest writers will be able to make this repetitive pattern book. Start by brainstorming a list of adjectives to describe dinosaurs. Then have each student think of the name of a dinosaur and an action word that goes with it (for example: *"A triceratops walks."*). This will be the first page of his book. On the next page, add an adjective to the sentence: *"A tremendous triceratops walks."* For each following page, the student adds another adjective to the sentence. Next the student illustrates his pages. Your students will be eager to take their booklets home to share with their families!

Dinosaur Diamante

Challenge older students to work with adjectives. Dinosaurs are the perfect inspiration for writing a form of poetry called a *diamante*. This five-lined poem forms a diamond shape. Model a diamante poem as shown:

first line: name of dinosaur
second line: two words describing what the dinosaur looked like
third line: three words describing what the dinosaur did or was
fourth line: two words that describe how the dinosaur makes you feel
fifth line: a noun that is a synonym for the word in line one

Have students write their diamantes on dinosaur-shaped paper (see the patterns on pages 92–95). Compile the finished diamantes in a booklet for your classroom library. Your students may surprise you with the vocabulary they have learned about dinosaurs!

Dinosaur Day

Culminate your unit with a day of celebration! Encourage students to bring dinosaur models and toys from home to inspire some hands-on fun.

"Sandwich-a-saurus"

Let your students really sink their teeth into this activity! Each student will need a piece of bread, a plastic knife, and a paper plate. Provide dinosaur-shaped cookie cutters; jars of peanut butter, jelly, and honey; and containers of raisins and nuts. To create edible creatures, the students use cookie cutters to cut shapes from the bread. Direct them to "color" their dinosaurs by spreading on the peanut butter, jelly, or honey with plastic knives. Add nuts and raisins to make eyes, teeth, spikes, etc. When the project is finished, you may be tempted to snap a picture before all of the "dinos" are devoured!

"Guess-a-saurus"

Enjoy the riddles in the book *Tyrannosaurus Wrecks* by Noelle Sterne (Thomas Y. Crowell Junior Books, 1979). Read several of the riddles to the class, or let students take turns reading the riddles to each other for some rib-tickling reptile humor!

"Student-a-saurus"

Your students' imaginations will go wild with this drawing activity. Ask students to think of a dinosaur they would like to be. Have each student draw a picture of himself as a dinosaur, using his face on a dinosaur body. The results are sure to bring smiles from everyone as they see the funny results!

"Pin-a-saurus"

Create a prehistoric pin to wear! Each student will need a one-inch ball of air-drying clay and a safety pin. Instruct each student to flatten the clay into an oval shape approximately 1/4-inch thick. Use objects such as chicken bones, fern leaves, or seashells to imprint a shape into the clay. Carefully press the safety pin into the clay as shown. Let the pins dry overnight, having the students turn them over before they leave for the day. What a fun keepsake of Dinosaur Day!

More "Dino-Mite" Reading
Your class will enjoy these books about dinosaurs:

Dinosaur Bob And His Adventures With The Family Lazardo
written and illustrated by William Joyce
HarperCollins Children's Books, 1988
   The Lazardo family finds a dinosaur in Africa and decides to bring it home to America with them.

Dinosaur Days
written by Linda Manning and illustrated by Vlasta Van Kampen
Bridgewater Books, 1993
   On each day of the week, a different dinosaur appears at a girl's house to engage in some sort of mischief.

If The Dinosaurs Came Back
written and illustrated by Bernard Most
Harcourt Brace Jovanovich, 1991
Have fun with this look at how dinosaurs would fit into today's society.

Lila's Little Dinosaur
written by Wolfram Hanel and illustrated by Alex de Wolf
North-South Books, 1994
   A little girl with a fondness for dinosaurs is amazed when one actually follows her home.

Spiny
written by Jurgen Lassig and illustrated by Uli Waas
North-South Books, 1995
   This chapter book follows a dinosaur who wanders too far from the nest and the concerned friends who try to help him get back home.

You Can Name 100 Dinosaurs! And Other Prehistoric Animals
written by becker&mayer! and illustrated by Randy Chewning
Scholastic Inc., 1994
   Look at pictures of many kinds of dinosaurs, complete with facts and explanations for younger children.

Pattern
Use with "Tracking Down Similes" on page 84.

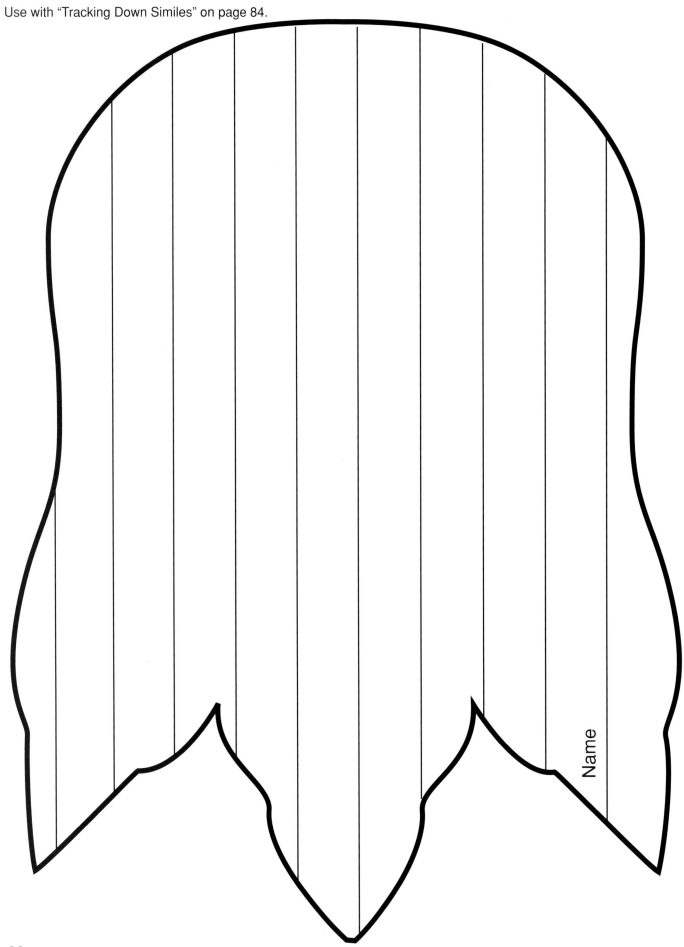

Name

How Big Were They?

Not all dinosaurs were *gigantic.* After reading about dinosaurs, use the graph below to show how long each dinosaur was.

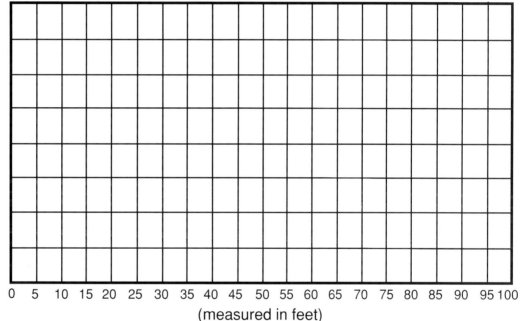

Corythosaurus

Fabrosaurus

Ultrasaurus

Iguanodon

Stegosaurus

Barosaurus

Triceratops

Tyrannosaurus rex

0 5 10 15 20 25 30 35 40 45 50 55 60 65 70 75 80 85 90 95 100

(measured in feet)

1. What was the biggest dinosaur on the graph?

   _____

2. What was the smallest dinosaur on the graph?

   _____

3. What three dinosaurs were the same size?

   _____, _____, and _____

Corythosaurus
(kor-rith-oh-saw-rus)

Corythosaurus

Triceratops
(try-ser-rah-tops)

Triceratops

Tyrannosaurus rex
(tie-ran-oh-saw-rus recks)

Tyrannosaurus rex

Barosaurus
(bar-row-saw-rus)

Barosaurus

Ultrasaurus
(ul-tra-saw-rus)

Ultrasaurus

Stegosaurus
(steg-o-saw-rus)

Stegosaurus

Oviraptor
(ove-ih-rap-tor)

Oviraptor

Deinonychus
(die-no-ni-kus)

Deinonychus

Pentaceratops
(pen-ta-ser-a-tops)

Pentaceratops

Gallimimus
(gal-ih-mime-us)

Gallimimus

Iguanodon
(ig-wa-no-don)

Iguanodon

Fabrosaurus
(fab-ro-saw-rus)

Fabrosaurus

Pattern
Use with "Dinosaur Diamante" on page 85.

Answer Keys

Page 23

1. risk taker
2. helpful
3. peaceful
4. conscientious
5. polite
6. honest

Other answers for character traits will vary.

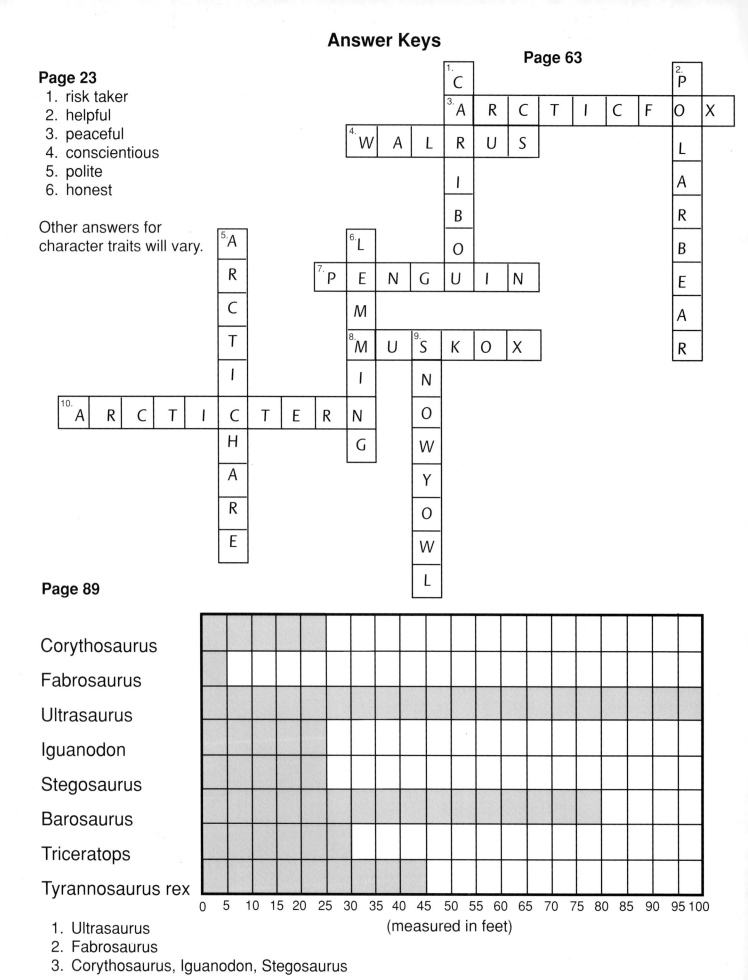

Page 89

1. Ultrasaurus
2. Fabrosaurus
3. Corythosaurus, Iguanodon, Stegosaurus